IN

Great men and women who lived and fought during the American Revolution wrote their memories in a book or a diary...they are called memoirs in our generation. What are memoirs? **Memoirs** are an historical account or a biography **written from personal knowledge** or special sources. I have painstakingly read the memoirs of a few great men; Professor Boyd Dawkins, Benjamin Franklin, Thomas Jefferson, William Penn, Private Daniel Flohr, Colonel Hugh Wynn and others. These memoirs contradict the fictitious (fiction or fake) History created by Academia and the History Channel. The memoirs of the men that I have listed above tell a story of 5 black armies that fought the American Revolution; black French troops, black German troops, black Polish troops, black Continental troops and black Officers. The memoirs in this book describe a black Haitian army that fought at Savannah Georgia and Yorktown....yes...these are nonfiction **(real)** memoires that can be proven. These memories describe **the black management of the American Revolution** on **both sides of the Atlantic!** On the Continental side there were black Presidents of the Continental Congress before and during the American Revolution. On the British side, King George the 3rd was black and so was the British Parliament. The British Prime Minister, Chief magistrate justice and Attorney General were black during the American Revolution. **The research in this book is founded on the memoirs** of people who were alive during and

Ms. Sonja C. Anderson
14266 Breakfast Dr
Redford, MI 48239-2909

immediately after the American Revolution. Most of the memoirs that you are going to be exposed to are from people who shed blood for the American cause and yet.....their memories are not permitted in the hallowed halls of academia. Why would Academia do such a thing? **Because these memoirs tell a story** that has never been heard with the hearing of the ears.....a story of.....**the black military occupation of the 13 colonies!** The black British/German/ Hessian troops occupied **New York 6 years, Charleston Sc 2 ½ years, Savannah Georgia 4 years** and **Boston 7 yrs** and yet.....this information has been blotted out from real World history! **The image on the front cover of this book depicts the black British/German army as they are destroying a statue of the German King, King George the 3rd of England.** The image is authentic and validates the words of **Benjamin Franklin** in which he **said," the Germans are swarthy/black!** The British hired over 30,000 black German/Hessian troops to put down the rebellion in the 13 British colonies. This is the reason why I charged Academia, the History channel, Hollywood and their museums with fraud. All of these entities have one thing in common...they teach false memories. These Government sponsored entities can't prove the authenticity of the history books that they write or the artwork that they display in their museums. These false memories are tools that the elite use to create artificial intelligence or a hybrid man. If you have read any of my work...you already know what this is....this is indeed the next episode!

MEMOIRS OF A BLACK AMERICAN REVOLUTION

PROFESSOR BOYD DAWKINS

OUR EARLIEST ANCESTORS PGS-96 & 97

"In the year 449 A.D certain Englishmen came from **North Germany, South of the Baltic Sea** and pushed the black Britain's/Basque westward into; Wales/Welsh, Westmoreland, Devon, Scotland, Cumberland and Cornwall."

The Romans placed a wall **(122 A.D)** in Britain to keep the marauding (white) barbarians out of the country. This wall was called Hadrian's Wall.

WINCHELL ALEXANDER

OUR REMOTE ANCESTRY

"These short black men (Pygmies) came from Atlantis, North Africa and they overran Europe."

PROFESSOR HUXLEY

THE IBERIAN RACE PG-332

"The black Basque/Iberian bones have been found all over Europe."

DR. ALBERT CHURCHWARD

ORIGIN & EVOLUTION OF THE HUMAN RACE PGS-12 & 13

"It was in Africa that these Pygmies evolved and from there they spread all over the World. North, East, South and West until not only Africa but **Europe,** Asia, **North America**, South America and Oceania were populated by them."

BENJAMIN FRANKLIN, ESSAY, AMERICA AS A LAND OF OPPORTUNITY 1751

"France, Italy, Russia, Germany, Sweden, Spain, Asia, Africa and America is swarthy/black."

JAMES ANDERSON

RIDDLES OF PREHISTORIC TIMES, PGS-57 & 58

"The Iberians in ancient times inhabited the Western and Southern parts of Europe. **The black Basque in Spain and France, the dark Welshman,** the Scotch and **the black Celts to the West** of the **Shannon River in Ireland,** as well as **the same kind of men in Britain** and Equitaine **in France.**"

All of these Scholars, Doctors and Professors have something in common....they **are all white educated Europeans** from different era's and yet **they all have the same testimony**. What is their testimony? The blacks were the original people of Europe, why is this so hard for the masses to grasp? Human beings **(human=homan=hama=hima being)** have been migrating across the Earth for 6000 years and hardly anyone is where they are supposed to be. You have whites who have migrated to Africa, Asia, North America and we know they were not the original people of these lands. By the time you are finished reading this book....you will never think the same again. I have a greater witness than this.....let's take a look at the genetic research on the next page.

GENETICS

Institute of Evolutionary Biology,

Barcelona Spain

Published in the Nature Journal, 2006

Author Dr. Charles Lalueza

"Genetic tests reveal that a hunter-gatherer who lived 7,000 years ago had the unusual combination of dark skin, dark hair and blue eyes."

CONTINUED:

"Two hunter-gatherer skeletons were discovered in a cave in the mountains of north-west Spain in 2006.The cool, dark conditions meant the remains (called La Brana 1 and 2) were remarkably well preserved. Scientists were able to extract DNA from a tooth of one of the ancient men and sequence his genome. **The team found that the early European** was most closely genetically related to people in <u>Sweden and Finland</u>, but while his eyes were blue, **his genes reveal that his hair was black or brown and his skin was dark." You have to remember that Dark is code word for black.** In future chapters you will see an image of **a black German Prince with blue eyes**.....the painting is late 19th century.

AFRICAN ANCESTRY

The blacks in America have suddenly developed an interest in being reunited with their family on the Continent of Africa. These interests have fueled a fury of research in the field of Genetics and thus far have yielded some extremely surprising results. I have looked at some of the research that was done by **African Ancestry, Washington D.C,** and it was astounding. <u>**The results showed that 30% of all African Americans D.N.A was traced back to Europe!**</u> I began to pay closer attention when I saw the results that the tests produced. Some of the European Nations that the African Americans D.N.A traced back to were identical to the research presented in the **Negro Question Parts 4 and 6.** The same Nation's that Benjamin Franklin said were black in 1751, are the same Nations that black D.N.A is tracing back to. What are the odds that the genetic research done in this generation would verify the words spoken by Benjamin Franklin 266 years earlier?

EUROPEAN NATIONS AFRICAN AMERICANS D.N.A TRACED
BACK TO:

ENGLAND
IRELAND
WALES/BRITAIN
SCOTLAND
RUSSIA
GERMANY
ITALY

If you are interested in contacting African Ancestry, here is their contact info; contact African Ancestry (202)723-0900, Washington D.C.

84TH ANNUAL MEETING OF AMERICAN ASSOC PHYSICAL ANTHROPOLOGISTS RESEARCH; STUDY PUBLISHED BIO RXIV SITE

DR. LAIN MATTHIESON-GENETECISTS AT HARVARD UNIVERSITY

"Ancient D.N.A makes it possible to examine populations as they were before and after adaptation. **Dark skinned (black people) arrived in Europe 40,000 years ago and retained their dark skin (black skin) far longer than originally thought.** The article goes on to say, "rather than lightening as previously thought **the first people retained their dark skin color.**"

PROFESSOR CHRIS STRINGER LEADING ANTRHOPOLIGIST AT NATIONAL HISTORY MUSEUM IN LONDON

"This research adds more surprises to the remarkable complexity of population relationships in ancient Europe through ancient D.N.A. **The research further concluded that these dark skinned (black people) were lactose intolerant!**

Do you know anybody that is Lactose intolerant? Try looking in the mirror....African Americans are lactose intolerant. What does this mean? It means that the Europeans are trying to correct the lies that they were taught. The D.N.A evidence along with the European eyewitnesses, prove that the founders of Europe and the 13 colonies were a black people. I have a greater witness than this....come and see.

9

DNA; LONDON WAS ETHNICALLY DIVERSE FROM START

By Pallab Ghosh, Science correspondent, BBC News

23 November 2015

The researchers plan to analyze more of the 20,000 human remains stored at the Museum of London. According to Caroline McDonald, who is a senior curator at the museum, "London was a cosmopolitan **(black and white)** city from the moment it was created following the Roman invasion 2,000 years ago."

Why did the researcher call London a cosmopolitan city? The black Britain's/Basque were in Britain long before the arrival of the Romans...the researcher's history has been distorted...as usual. When the white barbarians invaded Britain in 449 A.D, the black Britain's and the mulatto Romans were already there. This cosmopolitan society that the researcher boasts of consisted of the original black inhabitants of Britain (Basque), the black Jews who Vespasian deported in 70 A.D, the invading Romans and lastly... the invading whites. Jeremiah the prophet wrote (Jeremiah 16:19)," O Lord my strength and my fortress, in the day of affliction, the Gentiles shall come from the end of the earth and shall say, **surely our fathers have inherited lies**, vanity and **things wherein there is no profit.** " This saying has come to pass in the Negro Question book series; the Gentiles have indeed inherited lies!

THE FIVE BLACK FOUNDING FATHERS OF THE 13 COLONIES!

KING JAMES STEWART	KING CHARLES 1ST STEWART	KING CHARLES 2ND STEWART

KING JAMES 2ND	KING GEORGE 3RD

1607 VIRGINIA FOUNDED BY BLACK SCOTS, KING JAMES THE 1ST
1620 MASS/MAINE FOUNDED BY KING JAMES THE 1ST
1620 NEW ENGLAND FOUNDED BY KING JAMES THE 1ST
1632 MARYLAND FOUNDED BY KING CHARLES 1ST
1629 NEW HAMPSHIRE FOUNDED BY KING CHARLES THE 1ST
1636 RHODE ISLAND FOUNDED BY KING CHARLES 2ND
1638 DELAWARE FOUNDED BY KING CHARLES 2ND
1663 NORTH CAROLINA FOUNDED BY KING CHARLES 2ND
1636 CONNECTICUT FOUNDED BY KING CHARLES THE 2ND
1681 PENNSLYVANIA FOUNDED BY KING CHARLES 2ND
1663 SOUTH CAROLINA FOUNDED BY KING CHARLES 2ND
1664 KING JAMES 2ND/DUKE OF YORK FOUNDED NEW JERSEY
1732 GEORGIA FOUNDED BY BLACK GERMANS , KING GEORGE 2ND

JOSEPH RITSON

"The Highlanders are generally diminutive, with brown complexions, and almost always with black curled hair and dark eyes."

JOSEPH RITSON

"The Highlanders are generally diminutive, with brown complexions, and almost always with black curled hair and dark eyes."

The spreadsheet below is from a ships manifest that describes the black Highlanders as they are boarding prison ships. They are described as black men...I guess Ritson was right!

THE SCOTTISH HIGHLANDERS

FIRST	LAST NAME	AGE		REMARKS
GEORGE	SAMUEL	18		BROWN
JAMES	DONALD	20		BROWN
ANDREW	MATTHEW	20		DARK COMPLEXION
WILLIAM	JACKSON	19		BROWN LUSTY
DONALD	MCDONALD	58		SWARTHY
WILLIAM	**ROSS**	**36**		RUDDY
DUNCAN	CAMPBELL	16		DARK COMPLEXION
JOHN	CUNNINGHAM	32		BLACK, STURDY
HUGH	MCFEE	30		BLACK, LUSTY
DANIEL	DINGWELL	31		BROWN
JOHN	BOUIE	14		NUT BROWN
DUNCAN	ORE	14		BROWN
JAMES	REED	18		BROWN
GEORGE	HUME	30	WRITER	BLACK MAN

JACOBITE GLEANINGS FROM STATE MANUSCRIPTS, PG-48

AUTHOR, J.MACBETH FORBES, HARVARD COLLEGE LIBRARY

The only colony that was not founded by a black Scottish Highlander King was the Georgia colony; I have to mention this in my conclusion to close any gaps that the Government sponsored scholar might use against the truth. The Hanover Kings were of German descent and according to Benjamin Franklin's essay; the German Hanover's were a black people. Benjamin Franklin wrote this essay in 1751 and at that time….the black German, King George the 2nd was sitting on the throne of England and that is a fact. The original translators of the King James Bible (1611) made a statement in their introduction and it reads" So that, if on the one side we shall be traduced (If they lie on us) by Popish persons at home or abroad, who therefore will malign us, because **we are poore Instruments to make GODS holy Trueth to be yet more and more knowen unto the people, whom they desire still to keepe in ignorance and darknesse**."

This introduction to the King James Bible was written 406 years ago and it is still true today. To this very day we have been kept in darkness and abject ignorance. You don't believe me do you? Do me a favor, stop reading for a minute and go get your King James Bible to see if your introductory page is missing. The introductory page is missing from your Bible isn't it? This is what the ancient translator meant when he said," **Whom they desire still to keep in ignorance and darkness.**" If I had not shown you that this page was missing from your Bible…you would still be in darkness. On the next page I would like to present to you the memoirs (memories) of former English secret service agent, John Macky Esp. What you are about to read will change your life forever! Come and see.

MEMOIRS

OF THE

SECRET SERVICES

OF

JOHN MACKY, Esq;

During the REIGNS of

King WILLIAM, Queen ANNE, and King GEORGE I.

INCLUDING, ALSO,

The true SECRET HISTORY of the Rife, Promotions, &c. of the English and Scots Nobility; Officers, Civil, Military, Naval, and other Persons of Distinction, from the REVOLUTION. In their respective CHARACTERS at large; drawn up by Mr. MACKY, pursuant to the Direction of Her ROYAL HIGHNESS the Princess SOPHIA.

Published from his Original Manuscript; As attested by his SON

SPRING MACKY, Esq;

The SECOND EDITION.

PUBLISHED IN 1733 NICHOLS AND SONS: BOOK LOCATION, THE NEWYORK LIBRARY

A DESCRIPTION OF **THE JACOBITE ROYALS**; PRINCES, DUKES, EARLS AND NOBLEMEN OF THE SCOTCH/IRISH AND BRIT/WELSH

(1) Charles Lenos page-36, **Duke of Richmond**, son of Charles the 1st of Scotland. **Black complexion, much like King Charles.**

(2) John Lord Somers, pages 48, 49 & 50 late **Lord Chancellor** (1651-1716) **brown complexion.**

(3) Daniel Earl of Nottingham, pgs-25 & 26 **Secretary of State**, a tall **thin black man.**

(4) Charles **Duke of Somerset**, pgs-16 & 17 Master of the horses. Reign of Charles the second. **Black complexion.**

(5) John **Duke of Buckinghamshire** pages-19 & 20 Was Earl of Mulgrave in the reign of King Charles the 2nd. **Brown complexion.**

(6) Charles **Duke of St. Albans,** page 40, 1st son of Charles the 2nd. **Black complexion, much like King Charles.**

(7) John **Duke of Newcastle** page 35, Earl of Clare before the revolution. King William created this gentleman a Duke and gave him a garter. **Black ruddy complexion.**

(8) Heneage finch **Lord Guernsey** page 90, Brother of Earl of Nottingham and solicitor to King James the 2nd. **A tall thin black man**.

(9) Earl of Fever ham page 98, Took oath to King Williams. A **middle statured brown man.**

This description of the black Jacobite Royals, Scottish Highlanders and Black Britain's/ Welsh comes to us from **a very reliable source....the English Secret Service!** What would you call a man that was given false memories, a false name and a false past? I would call him **a hybrid, an artificial being** and that is what has happened to the so-called Negro. This hybrid Negro has forgotten his true history, his God and his land. The great switcheroo has taken place; someone else is living in your mansion, wearing your Royal titles, assuming your history and swatting on your land. They appear in Social media as the Royals of Europe when they know that this is historically and genetically impossible! We are the seed of the black Jacobite **(Israelite)** Royals of Europe. They allowed us to keep our Scott, Irish, German, French and British last names but our memories have been erased. Your memory is erased by the lies that they teach you in the Government sponsored school system.

THREE KINGS AT THE LUDGATE LONDON

This image found at the Bucklebury Bank of London shows the images of **three black Kings** and is dated to the year 1667. There are only three Scottish Kings that can fit this timeline; King James the 6th of Scotland (far right), King Charles the 1st of Scotland (center) and King Charles the 2nd of Scotland, to the left. The balls in the hands of the three Kings represent world ruler ship and the only Kings that took pictures with balls in their hands were the Byzantine Kings. These black rulers of Scotland, Britain, Ireland and England were Jacobites (Hebrew Israelites) and this will be proven perfectly in upcoming chapters! The Jacobite rebellion of 1715 and 1745 was a famous black history moment in European history....and we know nothing about it.

PROFESSOR BOYD DAWKINS

"**The inhabitants of Britain** belong to very different races; Britain was inhabited by **the black Basque** from ancient times and <u>in their books they **called themselves Britains and Roman citizens**</u>."

These images of the Stewart Kings (Scottish Highlanders) excavated at the Bucklebury Bank of London proves that King James and his seed were black. I have presented the facts as they emerged out of the ground along with the eyewitness accounts. It is time for you to put on the robe of a Judge and to sit in the Judgment seat. The only advice that I shall give to you is the words of the Christ," **Judge not that you be not judged <u>but if you Judge….Judge righteously.</u>**"

THE BLACK FOUNDING FATHERS OF THE 13 COLONIES

KING JAMES STEWART	KING CHARLES 1ST STEWART	KING CHARLES 2ND STEWART

KING JAMES 2ND STEWART	KING GEORGE 3RD GERMAN KING

King James the 1st, King Charles the 1st, King Charles the 2nd, King James the 2nd and the black German King George the 2nd are the true founders of the 13 British colonies. These black Kings are the real founding fathers of the 13 colonies, there is no such thing as" **the white founding fathers," it is a myth!** If you are a history teacher, social studies teacher or a pastor of a church I don't fault you for what you teach…you have been teaching what you were taught….**that is not your fault.** I believe that it was the Apostle Paul who said," When I was a child I spoke as a child (1 Corinthian 13:9-12) but when I became a man I put away childish things. **What we learned in the Government sponsored school system about European and Colonial history are false memories. Verse 12** for now we see through a glass darkly; **we have been looking at history through a dark glass…..**books and images **provided to us by the Texas State school board, they have mentally steered us away from the truth.** What is the conclusion of this great matter? **The whites have done a great job** of picking up the pieces and transforming the 13 colonies into a modern Superpower. This could not have been achieved without the aid of the black soldier, who has fought valiantly in all of America's wars. **The credit for the founding of the original Colonial Government and the 13 black British colonies must be given to the black Scots and Britain's.**

KING GEORGE THE 3RD OF ENGLAND

SCIENCE MUSEUM.ORG, UK

This is an accurate image of King George the 3rd the **black German King of England**. King George the 2nd legalized slavery in the state of Georgia in the year 1751 and King George the 3rd had the dubious distinction of being the King that lost the 13 black

19

Colonies. The data and research to support this last claim can be found in the **Negro Question Part 6- The 13 Black Colonies.** I would like to deviate from the subject of King George the 3rd and look at the policies of his father, King George the 2nd as it relates to the Slave trade. <u>We have been programmed with **false memories** of British slavery</u>....we have been taught that the British had slaves in the Southern States. We have been taught that the first slave came into Virginia in 1619.....this is not true. The black British/Scots were not involved in slavery nor did they own the Southern States....they belonged to the French and the Spanish. There is a peace treaty that is still being recognized by the U.S and England, called **the Paris Peace Treaty of 1783**...let's examine this peace treaty that was signed by King George the 3rd.

PARIS PEACE TREATY 1783

Article1:

His Brittanic Majesty acknowledges the said United States; <u>New Hampshire, Massachusetts Bay, Rhode Island and Providence Plantations, Connecticut, New York, New Jersey, Pennsylvania, Delaware, Maryland, Virginia, North Carolina, South Carolina and Georgia, to be free sovereign and Independent States; that he treats with them as such,</u> and for himself his Heirs & Successors, relinquishes all claims to the

Government, Propriety, and Territorial Rights of the same and every Part thereof.

King George never mentions; <u>Alabama, Florida, Mississippi, Louisiana, Arkansas, Kentucky, Missouri, Texas, Tennessee</u> and do you know why? **Because the slave states didn't belong to the British,** they belonged to the Spanish and French. The only British colony to have a legal charter legalizing the enslavement of other human beings was Georgia....named after King George the 2nd...**<u>if you live in Atlanta Ga...you should</u>** know **<u>this.</u>** Slavery was not legalized in Georgia by the British until the year 1751, which means slavery only existed in that state one hundred and fifteen years! The black Monarchs of Scotland and Britain were not involved in slavery nor its trade.....go back and read the original Charters....there is no mention of slavery! **The blacks not only ruled England (King George the 3rd) but they held positions as Prime Ministers, Chief Justice Judge, Mayors and Alderman, Navy Admirals and Brigadier Generals.** By the time we **(you and I)** are through examining the research in this book we will have to make a hard decision. We will have to decide whether we support **the Government sponsored narrative (memories),** <u>all blacks are descendants of slaves,</u> or the Memories of the people who were alive during the Colonial revolt. Let's open this discussion with the words of Professor Boyd Dawkins on the next page.

"When **we look at history over the past two to three years** we see that the claims of race have been those that have been advanced by Russia. She has assumed that she has the right to rule over all those of **the principle race of Russia** (black people). The **Germans** feel that they should rule over all the **Teutonic** (black Germans) people. Also if we look at what happened in France, (King Louis beheaded) Spain, (King abdicated throne 1808) and Italy we find that in those countries the cry of race has not been ignored. **There a dream has been shadowed forth to have one great Celtic empire to include France, Spain and Italy** so as to embrace under one umbrella all those of the Celtic race. This conversation includes the English in America and the English in Australia…the English all over the World."

This is the question that you should to be asking yourself ….why is Professor Boyd Dawkins memoirs of any significance? It is significant because **he gives us a timeline by which the black Governments of Europe are falling** and **he names them in the order that they fell!** This information is a critical piece of evidence because **it teaches** the student and the teacher **the correct World order** in the 19th century. I have proof that the so called Negro sat on the throne

22

of England until the 20th century but that is another book for another time. Now that being said let us get back to the black Government of England during the American Revolution.

BRITAIN IN THE HANOVERIAN AGE 1714-1837: AN ENCYCLOPEDIA, PGS 287-290

On pages 287 to 290 **King George 2ND court is described as Teutonic....**the word **Teutonic** was a word that described **all the Germanic tribes**.....and based on the writings of Benjamin Franklin a picture begins to emerge.....the Kings parliament was full of black people!

Professor Boyd Dawkins

OUR EARLIEST ANCESTORS PG-95

"Or suppose we go back a few years and examine **the history of Germany**. The cry under which the Germans have advanced to victory is the cry of a united Germany...**that Germany should unite under one rule all the Teutonic people."** The professor is referring to the black Holy Roman German Empire!

What color were the Germans in 1751? Let's rely on the eyewitness testimony of Benjamin Franklin.

BENJAMIN FRANKLIN 1751

ESSAY; AMERICA AS A LAND OF OPPORTUNITY

"GERMANY IS SWARTHY/BLACK"

The Colonial revolution started 25 years from the date of Benjamin Franklin's essay.....hardly enough time for the German people to go from being black to white! This book will prove that the black British/German army occupied the 13 colonies.

BENJAMIN FRANKLIN

"And **since Detachments of English <u>from Britain</u>** sent to America, will have their Places at Home so soon supply'd and increase so largely here; **<u>why should the Palatine Boors [Germans] be suffered to swarm into our Settlements</u>** and by herding together establish their Language and Manners to the Exclusion of ours? Why should Pennsylvania, founded by the English, become a Colony of Aliens, **<u>who will shortly be so numerous as to Germanize us</u>** instead of our Anglifying them, and will never adopt our Language or Customs, **<u>any more than they can acquire our Complexion?</u>**

When Benjamin Franklin arrived in the 13 colonies (1723), there was already a black Scotch/Irish, Dutch, Swede, German and Welsh population present in great numbers. These blacks were the seed of the original colonists who had come to North America in the days of King James the 6th of Scotland; King Charles the 1st, King Charles the 2nd and King James the 2nd/Duke of York. The data associated with the colonization of North America by these black Scots and black Brits can be found in the Negro Question Part 6-The 13 Black Colonies. This was the reason that Benjamin Franklin sounded the alarm in his essay. The **original colonists** were black, the **American Indians** were **black** and here comes another **70,000 black Europeans** (Germans and Scotch/Irish) pouring into Pennsylvania. See the black parliament on the next page.

CHARLES JAMES FOX

R.t Hon.ble CHARLES JAMES FOX ESQ.r

BRITISH STATESMAN AND FOREIGN SECRETARY

1806 LADYS MAGAZINE

(1) THE ATLANTIC MONTHLY VOLUME 105 , PG-447

"Charles Fox is a short fat and gross man with a swarthy complexion and dark eyebrows.

(2) MEMOIRS OF THE LIFE AND TIMES OF KING GEORGE THE 3RD

PG-388

"Fox's figure is broad and heavy, inclined to corpulence (obesity). His figure was harsh, **Swarthy (black)** and **Sanguine (ruddy)**. He looked like King Charles the 2nd of whom he was the great, great grandson. **The most striking feature on his face was his** black and shaggy eyebrows."

Charles Fox fits the eyewitness descriptions from two different sources....so tell me...whose report are you going to believe...the eyewitness or this modern historian? Lets' look at the description of King Charles the 2nd based on the eyewitness account of former English Secret Service agent John Macky.

THE MEMOIRS OF JOHN MACKY

"Charles,Duke of St. Albans, is son to King Charles the 2nd by Mrs. Gwyn, **he is of a black complexion much like King Charles.**"

WESTMINSTER WAX MUSEUM ENGLAND

This is a wax image of King Charles the second, the great grandfather of Charles James Fox....who was the first foreign secretary and a member of the whig party.....and yes he was black! **His pedigree is in his** name...he was named **Charles** after King

Charles the 2nd of England and then he was named **James** after his great grandfather King James the 6th of Scotland.

STATUE OF CHARLES JAMES FOX, 1749-1806

SIGNED L. GAHAGAN, DEC 1, 1798

LOCATION 10 DOWING STREET. ENGLAND

MEMOIRS OF GENERAL KEPPEL

THE EDINBURGH REVIEW, VOLUMES 143-144, PG-235

" A greater man than Robert Adair lives in Lord Albermales recollections (memories). **It must have been in the summer of 1806, when he was about 7 years old that his father took him to see Mr. Fox**. In many respects his personal appearance differed little from the many pictures and prints of him. **His face had lost its swarthy appearance, which in the caricatures of that day obtained him the name Niger**".

This is a credible eyewitness that knew Mr. Fox from the time he was 8 years old to his adulthood. This statue of Charles James Fox comes closer to the eyewitness account from General Keppel. The word Niger was an ancient name from antiquity that meant black....there was nothing derogatory about it. You can get a hint of this when reading the Bible (Acts 13:1); Now there was in the Church at Antioch certain Prophets and teachers; As Barnabas **and Simon called Niger! In fact in the year 193 A.D Pescennius Caesar was so black that they called him Pescennius Niger.** Charles James Fox Niger was the Secretary of State of Britain in 1782,1783 and 1806. This means that this black Britain **was the Secrtary of State during the American Revolution.** Do you remember what I said in my introduction? I said that the blacks managed the Revolutionary war on both sides of the Atlantic and we are now beginning to see the proof. **BLACK SECRETARY OF STATE GREAT BRITAIN.**

WILLIAM PITT 1759-1806

IMAGE LOCATION, NATIONAL PORTRAIT GALLERY

BRITISH STATESMAN AND PRIMEMINISTER OF ENGLAND

As you can see the former Prime Minister of England was depicted as a black man....not only in engravings but also in the caricatures drawn of him in his generation. Mr. Pitt was the black British Prime Minister of England during the American Revolution. **BLACK BRITISH PRIME MINISTER.**

CARICATURE OF WILLIAM PITT THE YOUNER AND KING GEORGE 3RD OF GREAT BRITAIN

BRITAIN POLITICAL CARTOONS OF 1780

What is the point? In this caricature King George the 3rd, Queen Sophia and William Pitt the younger are portrayed as a ruddy or sanguine skinned people. **The word sanguine** means deep red which is identical to the word ruddy, which also means red. This would come as no surprise to you if you knew that **King George and his wife, Sophia Charlotte, were black Germans** from Hanover Germany.

Where did William Pitt and his family come from? Let's allow Professor Boyd Dawkins to answer my question.

"Professor Boyd Dawkins said," **Britain was inhabited by the Black Basque/Welsh from ancient times.** In the year 449 A.D certain Englishmen came from North Germany and the Southern shores of the Baltic sea and **pushed the Britain's Westward** and later on Britain was renamed Wales/Walsh.

You have to remember that the Britain's began to be called Wales or Welsh after they were pushed westward. Before the whites invaded Britain the entire land mass was called Britain....never Wales.

<u>In the year 449 A.D certain Englishmen came from North Germany and the Southern shores of the Baltic sea and **pushed the Britain's/Welsh Westward.**</u> "The white Anglia pushed the black Welsh/Brits Westward into **<u>Wales,</u>** Cumberland, Westmoreland, Highlands of Scotland, Devon and **Cornwall.**"

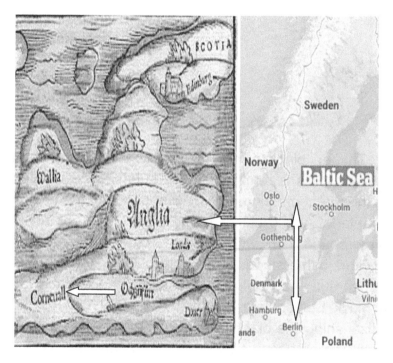

The Pitt's came from Cornwall located in the far West of Britain.....this man was black and his caricatures of that day present him as a ruddy man. See the next page.

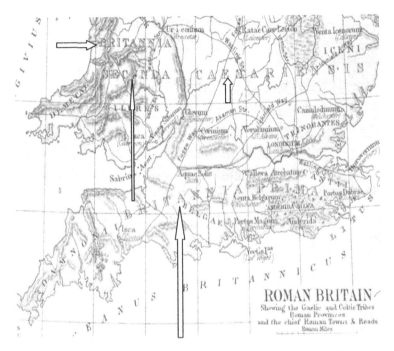

ROMAN BRITAIN
Shewing the Gaelic and Celtic Tribes
Roman Provinces
and the chief Roman Towns & Roads
Roman Miles

These black Britain's were indeed Roman citizens...this is reminiscent of Paul as he responded to the threat of being beaten without a trial. In the 22nd chapter of Acts (Acts 22:1-3,24 & 25) Verse 25 and as they bound him with thongs, Paul said unto the Centurion that stood by," Is it lawful for you to scourge a man that is a Roman and uncondemned? Paul was a black Benjamite Israelite and yet he had Roman citizenship. The black Britain's/Israelites were Roman citizens who became the founders of the 13 colonies. The seed of this black Roman/Britain is alive and well in the 13 colonies/America. In the books that the black Britain's left behind they called themselves Roman citizens.

JOHN WILKES, BRITISH PARLIAMENT

BRITISH MUSEUM, 1768

The Swarthy John Wilkes (Black Welshman) was elected as a member of Englands Parliament in 1757 and was also a former Alderman of London. During the American Revolution he was a supporter of the American rebels, boistering his popularity in the 13 colonies. I slowed the image down on the next page so that you could get a better glimpse of his blackness.

JOHN WILKES, BRITISH MUSEUM

John Wilke's was a Politician, Essayist, Journalist, MP and soldier. Mr. Wilke's owned a Newspaper called the North Briton! The document in his hand is a bill for Parlimentary reform. **BLACK PARLIAMENT.**

LORD NORTH

BRITISH POLITICAL CARTOON, 1775

JUSTICE MANSFELD, KING GEORGE THE 3RD AND LORD NORTH

Lord North was the black Prime Minister of Britain from 1752 to 1790 and he is depicted as a black man riding on the back of the Kings buggy. Lord North was the British prime minister during the American Revolution. **BLACK BRITISH PRIME MINISTER.**

BRITAIN POLITICAL CARTOON-1775

CHIEF JUSTICE MANSFIELD

DRIVING KING GEORGE AND LORD NORTH

Lord Justice Mansfield **(born Scone Scotland)** became Attorney General in 1754 and several months later he became Chief Justice of Great Britain. Lord Justice Mansfield is depicted as a black man in engravings, art and caricatures. He is perhaps best known for his judgment in the Somerset case of 1772. **Justice Mansfield ruled that slavery had no basis in common law and had never been established by legislation in England,** and therefore **was not binding law.** This is what I have been saying all along....the Black Kings of Scotland and England did not recognize slavery and that is the reason that the slavery verbiage (wording) is absent from the Colonial Charters. The Scottish people have been black from ancient times. **BLACK CHIEF JUSTICE.**

Black people had been taught self ruler ship by the best...the Most High God. When God came down on Mt. Sinai (Sinai=sayna=seen) he gave the Hebrews the tools of self Government; His statutes, his laws and his judgments. We took what God taught us and taught the rest of the World. In 1600 B.C the black Phoenician King Cadmus gave the Hebrew alphabet to the Greeks. The Ruddy **(red)** King David of Israel recorded the Hebrew alphabet in the 119th Psalm, between the years 1060 B.C to 1020 B.C. The alphabet below is the correct Hebrew alphabet that was used from Abraham to Jesus (YHSW). This alphabet appears on the coins and the manuscripts, which date from the time of the Prophets and the Apostles.

The images of the Hebrew Alphabet in your Bible (119th Psalm) are incorrect images. That alphabet is

39

the square alphabet of the Edomites who reside in Jerusalem. In 323 B.C the Greek Pharaoh Ptolemy requested that 72 Hebrew elders come to Egypt and translate the Holy Scriptures into Greek and they did. This Hebrew alphabet trickled down to the Latin speaking people (Etruscans) and from there it flowed to the rest of Europe. This is the reason that Paleo Hebrew is called the great fountain. **There is no such thing as the English alphabet or the English language** and the white European scholars know this. The black British were using an alphabet that consisted of **Hebrew, Latin, Greek and German long before the invasion of the whites in 449 A.D**. This means that the black Britains/Welsh taught the white barbarians their language. This language was called Walsh or Welsh, the whites took the land, the titles and the history of these black people. If you possess an alphabet you can legislate and if you can legislate...you can have Nationhood. This is what the black races have been doing for the last 6000 years...building Nations! If you don't believe me look on the Continent of Africa, there are currently 54 black Nations on the Continent that black people built. Let's get back to the argument at hand....King George's black Parliament.

HENRY GRENVILLE, 1712-1770

FORMER PRIME MINISTER OF BRITAIN

1763 MONTHLY MIRROR, FOUNDER, THOMAS BELLAMY

Henry Grenville not only became Prime Minister in Britain but here are the other positions that this man held in his lifetime; Treasurer of the Navy, 1st Lord Admiral and he became the prime minister in 1763. By the way the man is not two toned....there was an attempt to whiten the photo.

CHARLES PRAT, SECRETARY OF STATE, 1714-1794

ENGRAVER, JOHN FABER NATIONAL PORTRAIT GALLERY-D1200

This black Britain once held the positions of; Lawyer, Judge, Whig Politician, Attorney General and Lord Chancellor. The British Parliament that was managing the war effort in the Colonies was black...plain and simple. **BLACK SECRETARY OF STATE.**

The Right Hon.ble Brass Crosby Esq.r Lord Mayor and Rich.d Oliver Esq.r Alderman of London

MAYOR CROSBY AND ALDERMAN RICH OLIVER OF LONDON

LONDON MAGAZINE, 18TH CENTURY

BLACK ALDERMAN

43

ATTEMPT TO WHITEN

ATTEMPT TO WHITEN

QUEEN CHARLOTTE, WIFE OF KING GEORGE THE 3RD

NATIONAL PORTRAIT GALLERY

The closer you get to the Colonial revolution you begin to see images of the black Teutonic court of King George the 3rd. The ministers of King George's court were descendants of the black Royals of Wales and Scotland. Queen Charlotte Sophia, **the black German Queen of England,** came from Mecklenburg Germany and married the black German King George the 3rd of Hanover Germany. This means that the English Royals during the American Revolution were black along with their court...amazing! What did Benjamin Franklin say? The Germans are swarthy/black. **BLACK GERMAN QUEEN**.

CHAPTER 3: BRITAINS BLACK OFFICERS

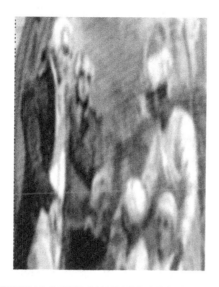

GENERAL LORD CHARLES <u>CORNWALLIS</u>

THE HISTORY OF THE WAR, FROM THE COMMENCEMENT OF THE
FRENCH REVOLUTION TO THE PRESENT TIME

VOLUME 1, AUTHOR HEWSON CLARK, PUBLISHED 1816

AND THE BRITISH MUSEUM

The black British General Cornwallis defeated Sultan Tipu of Mysore in May of 1791 but the actual treaty wasn't signed until March of 1792. The Sultan had to give his two sons to General Cornwallis as hostages until the treaty was signed. This teaches me something else....**that old proverb," <u>the Sun never sets on the British Empire,</u>"** it was these black British Generals who made this proverb possible. Professor Boyd Dawkins said," the Britain's were pushed westward into **Cornwall."** General **Cornwallis** was a black Britain and his last name is an indicator of where the man came from. The gentleman to the right of **Cornwallis** is none other than **Admiral Richard Howe** and if you strain your eyes you can see another black man behind Cornwallis. Though I can't prove it.....I believe the black man in back of General Cornwallis is none other than Commander and Chief of British armed forces.....William Billy Howe! **This black Britain, General Cornwallis, is the man that surrendered 8,000 Black/British/Hessian troops to the Continental army in Yorktown**. In fact New York was named after the Duke of York who eventually became King James the 2nd of England, there is an image of him on the next page. **BLACK BRITISH GENERAL.**

KING JAMES 2ND, THE DUKE OF YORK, DUKE OF ALBANY

BLACK JACOBITE KING OF SCOTLAND AND ENGLAND

1664 NATIONAL PORTRAIT GALLERY

This is undoubtedly what the prophet meant when he said, **"the people perish for lack of knowledge".** It is ironic that one of the most racist cities in the United States is the city of New York, which was founded by the black Scots, Dutch and French. One of the earlier founders of New York was a black Frenchman by the name of Nicolas Martiau; this man would become the great, great, great grandfather of George Washington. I shall hold on to this treat and give it to you in detail, in a later chapter. Let's get back to the black Parliament of King George. **BLACK SCOTTISH KING.**

ADMIRAL RICHARD HOWE

NATIONAL PORTRAIT GALLERY

ENGRAVER, JOHN SINGLETON COPLEY, 1794

(1) 1777 THE YEAR OF THE HANGMAN, PG-8

AUTHOR JOHN S. PANCAKE, UNIVERSITY OF ALABAMA PRESS

"THE TALL SWARTHY HOWE BROTHERS"

(2) ENCYCLOPEDIA BRITANNICA, A DICTIONARY OF ARTS
SCIENCES VOLUMES 13 & 14 PGS-837

"Admiral Richard Howe's nickname was
given to him on account of his **SWARTHY**
complexion. BLACK BRITISH ADMIRAL.

GENERAL WILLIAM HOWE

NATIONAL PORTRAIT GALLERY, ENGRAVER JOHN SINGLETON COPLEY 1794

(1) 1777 THE YEAR OF THE HANGMAN, PG-7

AUTHOR JOHN S. PANCAKE, UNIVERSITY OF ALABAMA PRESS

"THE TALL SWARTHY HOWE BROTHERS"

(2) THE AMERICAN REVOLUTION 100, THE BATTLES, PEOPLE AND EVENTS OF THE AMERICAN REVOLUTION, PG-58

"Commander William Howe was Swarthy, 6ft tall with bad teeth."

If you are a lover of history, you should only be concerned with the truth…not skin color. This is what Jesus (YSWH) told Pontius Pilate…"I came to bear witness to the truth."**BLACK BRITISH COMMANDER IN CHIEF.**

SIR HENRY CLINTON, K. B.

Commandant en Chef les Troupes
de Sa Majesté Britannique
dans l'Amérique.

IMAGE PUBLISHED BETWEEN 1770 AND 1780

BRITISH PRINTS AND LIBRARY OF CONGRESS

Sir Henry Clinton became Commander and Chief of the British army after the departure of Commander and Chief William Billy Howe. I have been unable to locate an eyewitness description of Commander Clinton but I am still trying. The Clinton Clan came from the Highland's of Scotland and this is the reason why he is depicted with a swarthy/black complexion. **BLACK COMMANDER IN CHIEF.**

LORD FRANCIS RAWDON, MARQUESS OF HASTINGS

WITH WASHINGTON AT VALLEY FORGE

BY WALTER BETRAM FOSTER PG-237

"**Lord Rawdon,** that **Swarthy** haughty nobleman, both hated and feared by all that came in contact with him was quartered to Peter Reeve's house."

This black man was Aide De Camp to the Commander and Chief of British armed forces and a Captain in the British army. <u>**Lord Rawdon was responsible for the purchase of Singapore.**</u> **BLACK AIDE DE CAMP TO HENRY CLINTON.**

BANASTRE TARLETON

1782 ENGRAVING, LIBRARY OF CONGRESS

PUBLISHED 1782, WALKER PATER, NOSTER ROW

AND WESTMINSTER MAGAZINE

WASHINGTON AND HIS COUNTRY

BEING IRVINGS LIFE OF WASHINGTON BEING ABRIDGED

PG-381

"This bold dragon **(General Banastre Tarleton)** so noted in Southern warfare, was about 26 years of age, **was of a swarthy complexion** with small black piercing eyes. **BLACK GENERAL.**

BRITISH GENERAL BANASTRE TARLETON

I cropped this image from the base of the statue on page 52 and blew it up so you could see the blackness of General Tarleton. The bottom portion of the image depicts a Swarthy, black and dark hued General Tarelton, which matches the eyewitness description of him and his men. General Banastre was suspected of massacring surrendering Continental troops at the battle of Waxhaw and thus he obtained the nickname...bloody Ban the butcher. **BLACK GENERAL.**

BLACK GERMAN GENERAL KNYPHAUSEN

General Knyphausen was a black German General from Hesse Kessel or Castle. When King George the 3rd hired the black Hessian mercenaries, the black Hessian officers came along to command these German troops. The Colonial troops were so undisciplined that the Congress enlisted the aid of Prussian (Germany) General Knyphausen. **Benjamin Franklin** said," The Germans are a swarthy/black people." **BLACK GERMAN GENERAL.**

MAJOR BENEDICT ARNOLD

BOOK, HUGH WYNNE THE FREE QUAKER, PG-385

"Major Arnold is a **DARK man** and **yet Ruddy** with a large nose".

HARPERS WEEKLY AND THE

CHICAGO TRIBUNE-09/19/1948 PG-324

"**A Swarthy** dark haired man, 5 feet 9 inches in height, **Arnold** was bold in speech and in action.

We have been deprived of our true role in the American Revolution......the black colonists and black Europeans managed the American Revolution on both sides of the Atlantic and I shall make that plain before we finish reading this book. **BLACK CONTINENTAL AND BRTIISH MAJOR.**

55

CHAPTER 4: FRENCH ROYALS & THEIR ARMY

15TH CENTURY PORTRAIT OF QUEEN ISABELLA OF FRANCE/BASQUE AND MORTIMER

BRITISH LIBRARY, ROYAL MS 14 EIV FOL.316V

Queen Isabella was the only surviving daughter of Phillip IV of France and **Joan 1 of Navarre**. Isabella married Edward 2 of England.....so as you can see the French royalty and its army were black from ancient times. On the next page I have provided you with an ancient image of King Sancho of Navarre and a medallion with Isabella's face on it.

Sancho I (circa 925 A.D.) King of Pamplona (Navarre). From Index of Royal Privileges, 12th-13th century manuscript.

The image to the right of Queen Isabella is that of King Sancho 1, King of Pamplona **(Navarre).** I'm showing you this image of the King of Navarre so that you could get a visual on what the people of Navarre actually looked like. These people were black from ancient times and the image of King Sancho 1 has been dated to 925 A.D. There is no disputing the blackness of Queen Isabella of France.

Volgens de Romeinse Copy. 1701.

KING LOUIS XIV/BASQUE AS THE SUN GOD APOLLO

FRENCH NATIONAL MUSEUM OF MONUMENTS, ABBEY OF SAINT DENIS

There is an interesting set of notes concerning the exhumation of King Louis XIV remains, not only was the body in good condition but King Louis was so black that they wrote in their notes, "**King Louis XIV skin looked like black ink.**" **BLACK FRENCH KING.**

PRINCESS LOUISE MARIE THRESA OF FRANCE/BASQUE

DAUGHTER OF KING LOUIS XIV AND MARIA THERESA

<u>MOOR OF MORET,</u> LIBRARY OF ST GRENVIEW, PARIS FRANCE

This image of Princess Louise Marie Theresa should give you an idea of the French Royal's blackness. Benjamin Franklin said," The French are swarthy/black." **The word Moor** meant black in medieval times and it still means black among the elite. It has been alleged that Secretary Tillerson called President Trump a Moron, the elite demanded an explanation and an apology but why? The word Moron is identical in context to the word Moor and in this generation Moron or Moor is code word for black or that other word! **BLACK FRENCH PRINCESS.**

MEMOIRS-THE DUC OF SAINT SIMON

THE COURT OF VERSAILES/BASQUE

ARROWS=FACES PAINTED WHITE

The entire court was Tawny with the exception of a few whites. I think that the word tawny (brown skinned) was the medieval word for mulatto or half breed. The Hebrew word taw means two and thus the word taw-ny implies two races combined. Thomas Jefferson said," **I saw 60,000 Frenchmen of all colors storming the Bastille." FRENCH COURT, TAWNY/BROWN.**

60

PROFESSOR BOYD DAWKINS

"The inhabitants of Britain belong to very different races; <u>Britain was inhabited by the **Basque**</u> from ancient times and **they called themselves Roman citizens**. In their books they were called the Britain's or Welsh; <u>there are two type of</u> **Basque/Welsh**, <u>one is **dark/black and 5 feet 4 inches** and the other is **tall and round headed**."</u>

The question was asked...who were these people and on page 103 **(of our Earliest Ancestors by Professor Boyd Dawkins)** <u>**the Professor states that the corpses (remains) of the Basque can be found in France,**</u> Ireland, **Britain**, Scotland, **Germany** (Rhine) Mediterranean, Spain, Portugal and **all over Europe!**

RIDDLES OF PREHISTORIC TIMES PG-58

AUTHOR JAMES ANDERSON 1911

<u>**The black Iberians in ancient times inhabited Western and Southern Europe,**</u> the Northern part of Africa and all parts reached from the Mediterranean Sea. **THE BASQUE IN SPAIN AND FRANCE**.

We have two different European Historians confirming that the original people of France were a black people called the Iberians or the Basque. This is how you get to the bottom of a long standing feud...not by arguing but by reviewing the available data. I used to hang out at a restaurant on the Westside of Chicago **(briefly)** where black preachers would congregate. They would come together to talk about God but they ended up arguing everyday and do you know why? These Ministers never carried a Bible! **If they had a Bible it would have killed the arguments** because they could have read the scripture themselves. <u>We could argue all day about the original color of the inhabitants of Britain, Germany and France.</u> If water puts fire out, then real hard evidence should end all arguing...right? You would think so but that is not the case. Those of us who walk among the young lions know that evidence means nothing to a blind man. When we were herded into the Government sponsored school system we thought that darkness was light because we had never been introduced to light. Let me take a few minutes of your time so that I can tell you a true story. One day the elders were reasoning among themselves and the question was asked," why do you suppose the Angels listened to the lies of Lucifer the fallen angel. One elder said," because he was the first Angel created" and another elder said," Because he was the light bearer." Neither answer satisfied the crowd of elders so they resumed arguing among themselves until at last an elder stood up in the midst and said," In the Kingdom of God there was no such thing as a lie....the Angels had never heard a lie and thus they believed their brother Lucifer and thus....darkness became light." The same thing happened to Adam and Eve...they had never heard a lie and just like the angels…they believed Lucifer! The same darkness that overthrew the angels and the first man Adam has overthrown this generation. **We have only been exposed to darkness**…two fold. When we enter into the Government sponsored school system darkness **(fiction)** awaits us; this is **the teaching of false memories** (World history) **that the United Nations cannot validate.** You didn't learn the truth in school so you go to the local Church and what awaits you? False memories, the churches are teaching a white Adam and Eve, Abraham, Moses and the prophets. The Churches have images of a white Jesus/YSWH and white Israelites…when they know that this is historically impossible.

CORNELL UNIVERSITY

Cornell University has learned how to split light around an object and poof… it looks like the object disappeared. The establishment didn't split light; **they simply burned the books that contained the light.** Academia doesn't have to worry about the things that they write nor the tainted images in their books. Academia sits as a Queen on a throne, her power and authority is absolute. There is no established platform to challenge the things that Academia teaches, the fix is in! Academia receives its power from the Prince of Darkness…Satan the Devil, the great deceiver.

KING CHARLES THE 5TH OF FRANCE

KING CHARLES THE 5TH OF FRANCE/BASQUE

HISTOIRE DE DU GUESCLIN, FRANCE

This is an image of King Charles the 5th of France and as you can see, he and the royal family are depicted as black people. Everybody in the image is black, including the knight who has a nappy afro. **BLACK KING OF FRANCE.**

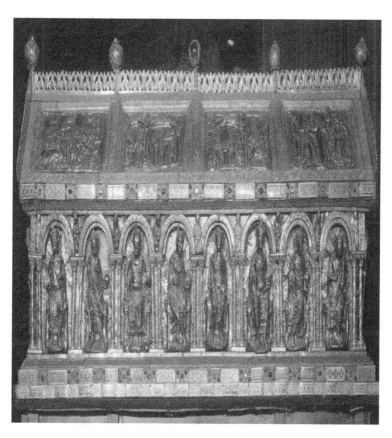

SHRINE OF CHARLEMAGNE

AACHEN CATHEDRAL, GERMANY 1215 A.D

When you look at this Shrine in its miniature form, you can barely see the jewels that are hidden on it but once you enlarge the images.....it is breathtaking. I've taken the liberty of blowing up the image on the next page.

Charlemagne Shrine - Commissioned by Henry IV, (1054). Palatine Chapel, UNESCO Site

KING CHARLEMAGNE, FRENCH BASQUE

IMAGE LOCATION, PALATINE CHAPEL, AACHEN GERMANY

I enlarged the image of Charlemagne so that you could see the blackness of this French King. This image fits the description of the black Basque that Professor Boyd Dawkins and James Anderson described. **BLACK FRENCH KING.**

These skeletal remains of 200 people were found beneath a supermarket in Northern France. The grave site was discovered by a company called Monoprix. Once the skeletal remains were found, the company called the French National Institute for Preventive Archaeological Research. On the surface it looks just like a bunch of skeletons but if you know what you are looking for then you realize the treasure at hand. I have enlarged the images of the skeletons on the next page.

The only people on Earth that possess wide nasal passages **(big noses)** are the black races and these skeletal remains found in France have the nasal passages of black people.

MEMOIRS OF THE LIFE AND WRITINGS OF BENJAMIN FRANKLIN PG-310

"On the road yesterday (France) traveling to Nantes, we met six or seven country women, in company on horseback and astride. Most of the men have good complexions, **not Swarthy, like those of North France and Abbeville.**

68

Take a wild guess, which part of France do you think these black skulls were found in? If you said Northern and Central France you just hit Lee's lottery! Let's examine the testimony of Thomas Jefferson concerning the blackness of the French people.

MEMOIRS OF THOMAS JEFFERSON

THE STORMING OF THE BASTILE

"60,000 FRENCHMEN OF ALL COLORS"

"The king of France came to Paris, leaving the queen in consternation for his return. Omitting the less important figures of the procession, I will only observe that the king's carriage was in the center, on each side of it the States general, in two ranks, afoot, at their head the Marquis de la Fayette as commander in chief, on horseback, and Bourgeois guards before and behind them **About 60,000 citizens (French Citizens) of all forms and colors."**

Thomas Jefferson gives an eyewitness **(memoirs)** account of the population in France during the French revolution. Thomas Jefferson was the Minister (Ambassador) to the French and he said," **The French were all colors.** Who are you going to believe... Thomas Jefferson, Benjamin Franklin or the guy writing 250 years later? I am throwing my hat in with the two witnesses; Benjamin Franklin and Thomas Jefferson. See the black French soldiers on the next page for the black French soldiers.

IMAGE TAKEN FROM TOP AACHEN PANEL

PALATINE CATHEDRAL, AACHEN GERMANY 1215

This is how you do it...you have to go back in time and find the artifacts, memoirs and eyewitness accounts <u>before the advent of racism</u> (1800) and then you will see the real history of the World. I have blown the image up on the next page so that you can see the true blackness of these French soldiers.

BLACK BASQUE/ FRENCH TAKEN FROM TOP OF PANEL, PG-70

PALATINE CHAPEL, AACHEN GERMANY 1215

These French soldiers fit the eyewitness account of the French National Museum concerning **the skin of King Louis XIV…"his skin is black as ink."**

71

FRENCH COMMANDER, CHARLES COMTE DESTAING

NEW YORK PUBLIC LIBRARY

This black Frenchman who fought valiantly on the side of the 13 colonies was to die a most horrible execution in his own land....France. During the French Revolution the black King, Queen, Admirals and commanders were beheaded or denied reentry into France. This was the tactic that Napoleon used to usurp power in France....the old lion and the young lions were denied reentry into France.

FRENCH GENERAL ALEXANDER DUMAS 1762-1806

IMAGE LOCATION WIKEPEDIA

This black man was one of the greatest Generals in the French army, second only to Napoleon Bonaparte. When Napoleon ordered his men to shoot the Negro nose off the Sphinx, General Alexander Dumas was there. **Napoleon had** been given **false memories**...he was taught that blacks had never accomplished anything...never built a civilization and had no history. When the **artificial** man, **Napoleon**, set foot in Egypt his **false memories** crumbled before the black statues of the Pharaohs. We have whites in this generation who are still trying to prove that the ancient Egyptian was white...when the word Egypt means black! **BLACK FRENCH GENERAL DUMAS.**

His response to racism,

"My father was a mulatto, my grandfather was a Negro, and my great-grandfather a monkey. You see, Sir, my family starts where yours ends."

Alexander Dumas was the son of the French General Alexander Dumas and he was hailed as one of the greatest writers in France's history. **Mr. Dumas** wrote **the 3 Musketeers, the count of Monte Cristo, the Vicomte De Bragelonnie and the knight of St. Hermine.** It is a statement that he makes in the last book that he wrote that bears investigating.

THE VICOMTE DE BRAGELONNIE AND THE KNIGHT OF ST HERMINE.

ALEXANDER DUMAS

"The first 10 years of my life was spent in the land of a mixed race people."

STOP! From time to time you are going to see eyewitness statements that you have read in earlier chapters but **it is necessary** to build a case for the research in this book....be patient...thanks.

"The French were Swarthy in Northern France"

In 1778 Benjamin Franklin was the Ambassador to France. This means that Franklin lived among the French people and he wrote **(memoirs)** what he saw….this makes Franklin an eyewitness.

MEMOIRS OF THOMAS JEFFERSON

THE STORMING OF THE BASTILE JULY 14, 1789

"I saw 60,000 Frenchmen of all colors."

Thomas Jefferson lived among the French people and he wrote **(memoirs)** what he saw….this makes him an eyewitness just like Franklin. Now that we have cleared this matter up let us proceed to one of the great secrets **(there are many!)** of the American Revolution. One of the secrets of the American Revolution is the fact that black German troops fought under the French umbrella.

ROYAL DEUX PONTS INFANTRY

DUKE GEORGE WILLIAM

COUNT PALATINE OF THE RHINE, ZWEIBRUCKEN BIRKENFIELD

WIKEPEDIA ENCYCLOPEDIA & BIRKENFIELD HISTORY 2

"**The Royal Deux Ponts Infantry was a German military outfit** that fought under the French umbrella; they were largely recruited from Zweibrucken Germany. **The "Royal Regiment of Two Bridges", commanded by the Comte Christian de Forbach, was part of a French Expeditionary Force that was sent to the United States to help it fight for its independence**. The Regiment was commanded by Comte Christian Forbach. His deputy commander was his brother and was **one of the four regiments that arrived at Newport** with Rochambeau in 1780. <u>**This regiment went on to participate in the Battle of Yorktown on the side of the Americans.**</u> Many of the soldiers came from the region around the city of Zweibrücken."

I have provided you with an image of George William Count Palatine of Zweibrucken himself....this is what the Germans looked like that fought under the French flag at York town ....yet there is no record of these black German Europeans! See the enlarged image below.

IMAGE TAKEN CROPPED FROM PAGE 76

This is what the German Duke, George Birkenfield, image looks like blown up. This simply means that the Royal Dux Ponts though fighting under the French flag were actually black Germans. This validates the words of Benjamin Franklin who declared, "The French and the Germans were swarthy". **Benjamin Franklin wrote this essay twenty four years before the American Revolution (1775)**. Twenty four years is not enough time for a people's skin color to change. In future chapters the white historians will testify that the French and German emigration totals were accidently added together because they looked identical....black.

THE HAITIAN REVOLUTION

HISTORIES DE NAPOLEON, M. DE NORVIN 1839 PG-239

This is another secret of the American Revolution **(there are many) In the American revolutionary war 4000 free black Frenchmen** (800 were riflemen) **who supposedly came from <u>Haiti</u>** fought on the side of the American Colonists in its revolt against the English. **<u>This all black (Haitian) unit fought in the</u>**

battle of; Savannah Georgia, Charleston South Carolina 1780, Pensacola, Sarasota Florida 1781 and Yorktown in 1781. The number allotted by the historians place the black free Haitian soldiers at 500. **This means that the French had in their army over 5000 black German and Haitian soldiers. General Cornwallis surrendered 8000 black German Hessian/British troops at Yorktown.** Do we have any memoirs that describe the soldiers that fought at Yorktown? Yes we have the memoirs of German Private George Daniel Flohr.

THE JOURNAL OF GERMAN PRIVATE, GEORGE DANIEL FLOHR

THE BATTLE OF YORKTOWN

"Three days later, on the morning of October 18, the articles of capitulation of **the English army, British/Germans,** in Yorktown were signed. The defeated army marched out that afternoon, and the **Royal Deux Ponts, German/French, held the place**

PG-76 GERMAN DUKE
GEORGE WILLIAM
ROYAL DEUX PONT

of honor among the French troops present. Afterward the troops were freed to inspect the damage they had inflicted. Flohr was horrified: **"Everywhere dead bodies lay around unburied, they were mohren/black.** Mohren comes from the word moor which means black!

79

What armies fought at Yorktown? The Germans, French, Haitians, Scotch/Irish, British/Welsh and the American colonists. These are all the Nations who Benjamin Franklin said were swarthy/black in 1751 and now you have a soldier, **George Flohr, who was present at Yorktown** saying…these Nations of men were black! **Who am I supposed to believe this modern historian or the eyewitness?** It's a no brainer; I got to go with the eyewitness. The establishment has the usual party line for us and do you know what that is? These black soldiers were freed slaves or runaway slaves; they were fighting for their freedom. This is always the establishment narrative when they see blacks with guns during the colonial era. The establishment narrative is illogical and it makes no sense. You beat this black man, raped his woman and sold his children into slavery. Would you turn your back on this angry black man if he had a gun in his hand? The narrative is illogical and it makes no sense? Listen to the warning that Pharaoh Kamose (Exodus 1:8-10) from the 17th dynasty of Egypt gave to his people," Come on, let us deal wisely with them **(Israel);** lest they multiply and it come to pass, that **when there is a war they join also unto our enemies and fight against us and so get them up out of the land.** If Pharaoh Kamose was alive today he would tell you the same thing that I am telling you….the narrative from the establishment makes no sense. Have you forgotten the John Brown massacre, Stono rebellion and the many slave rebellions in the South…think!

CHAPTER 5:   BLACK GERMAN HESSIAN STATE

It is a known fact among the so-called scholars that there were only 5000 inhabitants in Pennsylvania in the year 1723. This number included; Germans, Scots, Irish, Welsh/Briain's and English. In 1753 **(30 years later)** there were 40,000 black swarthy Germans in Pennsylvania along with 30,000 black swarthy Irishmen. This is why Franklin freaked out....the original colonists were black and now you have 70,000 black Europeans **herding into Pennsylvania."** You might think the writer is delusional....**but before I am through writing this book the proof will astound you.** If you were shocked by the black French and Haitian omission, you will be horrified by the omission of the black German troops. Let us examine the original draft of the Declaration of Independence and the words of Thomas Jefferson. See the next page.

THOMAS JEFFERSON

"They **(Great Britain)** too have been deaf to the voice of justice & of consanguinity **(common blood)** & when occasions have been given them, by the regular course of their laws, of removing from their councils the disturbers of our harmony, they have by their free election re-established them in power. At this very time too **they are permitting their chief magistrate**....................

CHIEF MAGISTRATE AND CHIEF JUSTICE

CHIEF JUSTICE MANSFIELD

......**to send over** not only **soldiers of our common blood but Scotch & foreign mercenaries to invade & deluge us in blood.**

King George sent over black Scots, Black Britain's and black German troops. As you can see the Chief Justice at this time was Lord Mansfield...a black man!

THE RELIEF PIAZZA, COLONINA ROME ITALY

COLUMN OF MARCUS AURELIUS

This relief depicts the marcomannic wars between the Romans and the black Germans (166 A.D-178 A.D). **These black Germans are the mercernaries** that Thomas **Jefferson is referring to** when he says, " they are sending over mercernaries to deluge us in blood." I have slowed the image down on the next page so you could see the true blackness of these German mercernaries.

IMAGE BLOWN UP OF BLACK GERMANIC TRIBES

These are authentic images of the black Germans and they fit the description given by Benjamin Franklin, **" the Germans are swarthy/black."** The Romans not only gave you a good beating but they did something else that is critical to **real history**....they always took a picture of the Nation whose head they were busting. When Vespasian Caesar destroyed Jerusalem in 70 A.D, he made the black Jews sit for a group photo before carting them off to Rome. If it had not been for this egotistical penchant **(habit)** of the Romans....we never would have known that the Jews of the New Testament were really black. You can find the images and the research in the Negro Question Part 3, The Black Pentecost.

3RD CENTURY FRESCO

DURA EUROPOS SYNAGOGUE, SYRIA

The Dura Europos Museum in Syria has the original black images of; **Moses, Abraham, Issac, Joseph, King David, Ezekel, Samuel, Isaiah and the prophets. These images have been carbondated to be over 2300 years old!** You will be horrified to know that this Museum or synagogue is currently being destroyed by rebels. I have used the images from this Museum/synagogue in the Negro Question Part 5, Joseph and the 12th Dynasty of Egypt.

COLUMN OF MARCUS AURELIUS, 3RD CENTURY A.D

BLACK ROMANS INVADE BLACK GERMANIC NATIONS.

The Germans were black in 166 A.D, the 3rd century and in 1751.

BENJAMIN FRANKLIN 1751, CONT'D

"the Germans, French, Italians, Russians, **Swedes, America**, Africa and Asia are Swarthy or black."

The Hessians/Germans were black from ancient times. When I first read this statement from Benjamin Franklin, I gloated over the blackness of the European

Nations but it was not until I began to write this book that the magnitude of this great lie finally set it. what lie am I referring to? We have been mentally steered toward the Continent of Africa by this statement, "**all blacks came from Africa."** This statement makes it virtually impossible for the black Hebrew elders to accept the fact that blacks were situated Worldwide. These old timers in Israel teach that the blacks went into Egypt on ships......they teach that Israel would be scattered into every Nation under the sun but it appears that they don't believe their own report. The brothers and sisters who have put the work in and have found out the secret of the Gentiles **(there are many secrets)** are eyewitnesses to the truth but the old timers refuse to believe their report. How can this be? We believed their report and they had less data to work with....this is not good. It is written in the scriptures," **the Gentiles will tell God that our fathers inherited lies,"** if that is the case and it is....**why do the elders continue to teach from the Gentiles history books?** Every man is taught of his father and mother...this was true in ancient times and this is true in our generation. If the Gentile's father taught false memories to his son....what do you think his son is teaching to our sons and daughters? **He is teaching our children the same false memories** that he learned from his father. These same false memories are then recorded in history books and sent into the World. We have elders in Israel proudly quoting false memories from the Gentile history books... every sabbath day...this is not good!

**BLACK GERMAN CHARLES OF BIRKENFELD, ZWIEBUCKEN
HISTORY OF BIRDENFELD & WIKEPEDIA COMMONS**

These black Germans were called Teutons **(two-tan)** and were located off the East coast of Britain.

PHILLIP 1 LANDGRAVE,COUNT OF HESSE, CIRCA 1535
PINTEREST

This is what a black German Hessian soldiers looked like and I would argue this with any of their scholars.

PRINCE MAURICE LANDGRAVE

PLATE FROM BIBLOTHECA CHALCOGRAPHICA, 1650

This image is that of Prince Maurice Landgrave Hessen, this is what an authentic German Hessian looked like that fought in the American revolution.

Not only did the black German Hessians send over 16,000 black troops to invade the 13 colonies as mercernaries, they also sent black German officers. Over 30,000 black German Hessian troops fought on the side of the British during the American revolution.

PARADOX

Black Germans fought under the French flag and then were forced to fight agains the black German mercernaries that the English had hired.....think about it! This will prove to be a black on black affair.

BLACK HESSIAN GERMAN DRUMMER

WIKEPEDIA ENCYCLOPEDIA

91

LANDGRAVE WILLIAM OF HESSE KASSEL

MAUSOLEUM, RUPENHEIM GERMANY

This is the King of Landgrave Germany, William of Hesse Kassel **(in Hebrew it means castle)** this is what the black British/German/Hessian soldiers looked like when they invaded the 13 colonies. This picture of a black, blue eyed Hessian Prince comes to within 4 years **(1787-1783=4)** of the end of the American Revolution. **The Germans were still black 4 years after the Treaty of Paris was signed.** If you take a look at the date in the top right hand corner of this picture you will see that **this black, blue eyed German didn't die until 1867! The Germans were still swarthy/black going into the 20th century…**this secret **(there are many secrets)** has been dealt with in the Negro question part 4, The Missing Link.

GENETICS

INSTITUTE OF EVOLUTIONARY BIOLOGY

BARCELONA SPAIN

Published in the Nature Journal, 2006

Author Dr. Charles Lalueza

"Genetic tests reveal that a hunter-gatherer who lived 7,000 years ago <u>had the unusual combination of dark skin, dark hair and blue eyes.</u>" Consider this next admission by the establishment.

84TH ANNUAL MEETING OF AMERICAN ASSOC PHYSICAL ANTHROPOLOGISTS RESEARCH; STUDY PUBLISHED- BIO RXIV SITE

DR. LAIN MATTHIESON-GENETECISTS AT HARVARD UNIVERSITY

"Ancient D.N.A makes it possible to examine populations as they were before and after adaptation. **<u>Dark skinned (black people) arrived in Europe 40,000 years ago and retained their dark skin (black skin) far longer than originally thought.</u>** The article goes on to say, "rather than lightening as previously thought **the first people retained their dark skin color.**"

PROFESSOR CHRIS STRINGER
LEADING ANTRHOPOLIGIST AT NATIONAL HISTORY MUSEUM IN LONDON

"**The research further concluded that these dark skinned (black people) were lactose intolerant.**"

The so called African American is lactose intolerant! The appearance of blue eyes on the portraits of black Princes and Generals coincide with the timeline that Professor Boyd Dawkins gives, for **the falling of the black Nations in Europe.** When the black British General Cornwallis surrendered 8,000 black troops to the Continental army it was said," that the world was turned upside down."

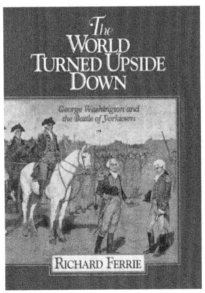

94

Think about this...234 years ago the black British General Cornwallis, surrendered 8,000 black troops to the Colonists; **Germans, French, Welsh, Irish and Britains.** The images of this black international army has been lost to mankind...**or so they thought.** I have managed to secure images of this black international cadre of soldiers as they are disembarking the British war ships. I thank God for the memoirs of Private George Flohr but the estalbishment would have us to think that only one man out of 8,000 had the presence of mind to keep a diary...this is illogical. Where are the other memoirs and the pictures that describe the Nations which fought the American Revolution? The coverup is real and you will see that by the time you are finished examining the research that I have provided for you. Come and see!

ARTICLE

THE FOUNDATION OF BRITISH STRENGTH, NATIONAL IDENTITY AND THE BRITISH COMMON SOLDIER, FLORIDA STATE LIBRARY

TO VIEW THIS WIKEPEDIA ARTICLE- TYPE HESSIAN IN GOOGLE BAR AND VIEW ARTICLE

"God damn you, Frenchy, you take our pay!" **The outraged Hessian replied: "I am a German** and you are a shit." This was followed by an impromptu duel with hangers, in which the Englishman received a fatal wound. The chaplain records that General Howe pardoned the Jaeger officer and issued an order that "the English should treat the Germans as brothers." This order began to have influence only when "our Germans, teachable as they are" had learned to "stammer a little English." Apparently this was a prerequisite for the English to show them any affection."

The reason the Englishman couldn't tell the difference between the French and the Germans is simple...they were both black! Let us consider the lineage of **the Howe brothers,** British Navy admiral Richard Howe and British Commander in Chief William Howe. These men were the sons of Emanuel Howe the 2nd Viscount and Sophia Charlotte. This lineage stretches backwards in time to the bloodline of King James the 6th of Scotland and Ernst Augustus, the king of Hanover Germany.

KING JAMES THE 6TH OF SCOTLAND

NEW COLLEGE LIBRARY, EDINGBURGH UK

NATIONAL PORTRAIT GALLERY

This is an authentic image of King James the 6th of Scotland and the 1st of England. Yes....this is the same King James that translated the Christian Bible. King James had a daughter by the name of Elizabeth Stewart who married Frederick the 5th of Bohemia, Germany. I have provided images of Frederick the 5th on the next page with an image of his wife Elizabeth Stewart.

Elizabeth of Bohemia (1596-1662) daughter of King James VI of Scotland and I of England and Ireland, mother Anne of Denmark. The wife of Frederick V, Elector Palatine (Holy Roman Empire), briefly Queen of Bohemia. Due to her husband's short reign in Bohemia, Elizabeth is often referred to as the Winter Queen. With the demise of the Stuart dynasty in 1714, her descendants, the Hanoverian rulers, succeeded to the British throne.

(1) FREDERICK THE 5TH OF BOHEMIA GERMANY

ENGRAVER, WILEM JAKOBSZ DELFF

(2) QUEEN ELIZABETH STEWART

ANCIENT MISC, SAXONY COINS

Read the story on the next page.

KING FREDERICK 5TH OF BOHEMIA GERMANY	QUEEN ELIZABETH STEWART OF SCOTLAND

IMAGES TAKEN FROM PG-98

I blew the image up so you could get a real good look at this black Bohemian King of Germany and his black Scottish Queen. So far Benjamin Franklin and Professor Boyd Dawkins have hit the nail on the head. **This marriage will eventually produce a little black Princess** who was known as **Sophia of the Palatinate. <u>Sophia married Ernst Augustus, King of Hanover.</u>**

STATUE OF THE BLACK GERMAN- ERNEST AUGUSTUS,
ELECTOR OF BRUNSWICK

MARIAN CASTLE, LOWE SAXONY GERMANY

Elector of Hanover, Ernest Augustus, the father of **King George the 1**st had an **illegitimate daughter by the name of Baroness Charlotte Von Platen**. In 1701 the Baroness who later became Countess Sophia, married Johan Von Adolf Kielmansegg. From this union was born a daughter by the name of Mary Sophia Charlotte Kielmansegg. It was this Charlotte Von Kielmansegg that married Emanuel **Scope Howe**

2nd Viscount. This marriage would **produce two German/Scottish princes, Admiral Richard Howe and Commander in Chief William Howe.** The Howe brothers fought on the British side during the American Revolution.

| ADMIRAL RICHARD HOWE | GENERAL WILLIAM HOWE |

NATIONAL PORTRAIT GALLERY

ENGRAVER, JOHN SINGLETON COPLEY, 1794

1777 THE YEAR OF THE HANGMAN, PG-7

AUTHOR JOHN S. PANCAKE, UNIVERSITY OF ALABAMA PRESS

"The tall swarthy and black (German/Scot) Howe brothers; Sir Billy and black dick".

(1) Encyclopedia Britannica, dictionary of arts and sciences, volume 13 and 14, PG-837, Admiral Richard Howe.

Admiral Richard Howe

Was nicknamed black dick on account of his swarthy appearance!

(2) THE AMERICAN REVOLUTION 100, THE BATTLES PEOPLE AND EVENTS OF THE AMERICAN REVOLUTION, PG-58

BRITISH COMMANDER IN CHIEF WILLIAM BILLY HOWE

"Commander William Howe was Swarthy, 6ft tall with bad teeth."

Admiral Richard (Prince) Howe is best known for his service during the American Revolutionary War where he acted as a naval commander and a peace commissioner with the American rebels. Admiral Howe also conducted a successful relief during the Great Siege of Gibraltar in the later stages of the War. At the beginning of the American Revolution, Howe was known to be sympathetic to the colonists. He had known Benjamin Franklin since late 1774 and was joined in a commission with his brother, General William Howe, head of the land forces to attempt reconciliation. We have a black German Admiral and a black Commander in Chief (William Howe) who commanded land and sea units....yet.....their black images have never seen the light of day in the Government schools. **The strategy of the British in North America was to deploy a combination of operations aimed at capturing major cities** and a blockade of the coast. In combined operations involving the army and the Navy the British took Long Island and captured New York City in 1776. In 1777 Howe provided support to his brother's <u>operation to capture Philadelphia</u>, ferrying General Howe's army to a landing point from which they successfully marched and took the city. Howe spent much of the remainder of the year concentrating on capturing forts Mifflin and Fort Mercer so that he could control the Delaware River. News of the capture of a separate British army under General John Burgoyne threw British plans into disarray. Howe spent the winter in Newport Rhode Island. They got the storyline right......but they somehow failed to include the black images of the Howe brothers and their soldiers! I suspect that I have your undivided attention by now, so let's proceed to the next chapter....the swarthy memoirs. This next chapter will introduce the reader to memoirs of people who were actually present during the American Revolution. You will read memoirs of people who actually saw or knew George Washington, Thomas Jefferson, Benedict Arnold and other important people from that era.

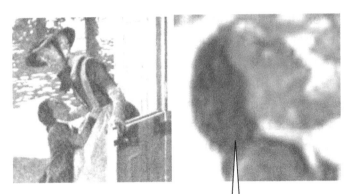

LT. COLONEL HUGH WYN, AS AN 8 YEAR OLD CHILD

BOOK, HUGH WYNN THE FREE QUAKER, PG-24

REFERENCE BOOK

COLONEL HUGH WYNE, BY SILAS WEIR MITCHELL PG-125

"We all rose as he drew near, my mother saying in my ear as he approached; "now Hugh, it is Arthur Wynn, now Hugh take care. **This newly found cousin was like all of us** (Wyne family) tall but not as broad as the other Wynn's, **he was of a swarthy** complexion....**his hair was coarse** (nappy) not fine.

COLONEL HUGH WYNE BY SILAS WEIR MITCHELL PG-8

WILLIAM JOHN PENN

"The lad looks like his people, **When you are a man my lad you will go back to Wales** to see where your people come from".

"Thomas Hickey, who has been described as 'a dark-complexioned man of five feet six, well set … an Irishman and hitherto a deserter from the British Army."

George Washington felt he needed security guards to protect his life so he **formed the life guard** or the commander and chief guard. One of the men, Thomas Hickey, was involved in a plot to assassinate and kidnap George Washington. Hickey was himself jailed by American authorities for attempting to pass counterfeit notes, and he unwisely talked of the plot with a cellmate, another counterfeiter named Isaac Ketchum, who was from Cold Spring Harbor."Ketchum, seeing an opportunity to be set free, squealed on Hickey. The ex-guard was court-martialed and found guilty of mutiny and sedition. On orders from Washington, and with 20,000 Continental soldiers as spectators, Hickey was hanged on June 28 in a field near Bowery Lane. **Swarthy continental officers continued on next page.**

"There he is, at this moment, riding up the hill from his quarters in the valley. **A man of medium height and strong frame, he sits his horse well and with a dashing air. His nose is prominent, his eye piercing, his complexion ruddy,** he has in him the qualities of a great general, as he shall show many a time in his short life of one-and-fifty years, **General Anthoney Wayne."**

IMAGE OF GENERAL WAYNE WITH HIS FACE PAINTED WHITE; THE HOCKEY MASK!	THIS IMAGE FITS THE EYEWITNESS ACCOUNT OF THE EYEWITNESS

STONY POINT MEDAL, BRIGADIER GENERAL ANTHONY WAYE, 1779

BLACK CONTINENTAL GENERAL.

BRIGADIER GENERAL MUHLENBERG

GENERAL MUHLENBERG A
BLACK GERMAN
CONTINENTAL

SHANDANDOAH VIRGINIA COURTHOUSE

MEMOIRS OF HENRY ARMITT BROWN

TOGETHER WITH FOUR ORACLE ORATIONS PG-329

"At the corner of the entrenchments by the river, is the Virginia Brigade of Muhlenberg. Born at the Trappe close by and educated abroad, **Muhlenberg was a clergyman in Virginia** when the war came on, but he has doffed his parson's gown forever **for the buff and blue of a brigadier. His stalwart form and swarthy face** are already as familiar to the enemy as they are to his own men, for the Hessians are said to have cried, 'Hier kommt Teufel Pete!'"

In English, 'Hier kommt Teufel Pete means...tough Pete is coming! Brigadier General Muhlenberg was a black German Continental officer. Benjamin Franklin told us that the German's were swarthy...the dots are beginning to connect! **BLACK GERMAN CONTINENTAL GENERAL.**

107

BRIGADIER GENERAL FRANCIS MARION, FRENCHMAN

(1)   MEMOIRS OF HENRY ARMITT BROWN
TOGETHER WITH FOUR ORACLE ORATIONS PG-329

(2)   A FEW BLOODY NOSES THE REALITIES

AND MYTHOLOGIES OF THE AMERIAN REVOLUTION

IMAGE-SOUTH CAROLINA VIRTURAL LIBRARY

IMAGE WIKEPEDIA

"Marion <u>was a stranger to the officers and men, and they flocked about him to obtain a sight of their future commander,"</u> recalled William James, who joined Marion's men when he was only 15. "<u>He was rather below the middle stature, lean and swarthy (Swarthy means Black).</u>

(3) JOURNAL OF MILITARY SERVICE INSTITUTION U.S JOURNAL
VOLUME 1 PG- 265

"General Marion was below middle size, lean and **swarthy, his French** betokened unmistakably his **Huguenot ancestry." BLACK FRENCH GENERAL.**

GENERAL JOHN SULLIVAN

MEMOIRS OF

HENRY ARMITT BROWN

TOGETHER WITH 4 HISTORICAL ORATIONS, PG-329

YALE UNIVERITY

"**Swarthy** John Sullivan is a little headstrong but brave as a lion." **BLACK SCOTTISH CONTINENTAL GENERAL.**

General John Sullivan was a black Scotch/Irish General that fought on the American Continental side during the Revolution. The Scot/Irish were black from ancient times.

CAPTAIN PAUL JONES

MEMOIRS OF THE MARQUEE OF ROCKINHAM

AND HIS CONTEMPORARIES, VOL 2, PG-379

"An adventurer with a single ship caused an almost consternation in the North. I mean **Paul Jones.** This celebrated renegade **from Scotland** was a short thick set man with **coarse** (coarse-medieval word for nappy) **features and swarthy complexion.**"

Captain Jones is a black Scotch/Irish with coarse (nappy) hair. **BLACK SCOTTISH CONTINENTAL OFFICER.**

CAPTAIN PAUL JONES

APPLETONS MAGAZINE, VOL 6, PG-116

MADEMOISELLE TELLISON

ARROW=WHITE PAINT

"Captain Paul Jones hair and eyebrows are black and his eyes are large, brilliant, piercing....**his complexion is Swarthy**...almost **like that of a Moor."**

Mademoiselle Telison states that this man was so black that he looked like a Moor....how can you be black and look black? There was an attempt to paint the image white....see the arrows.

111

GENERAL CHARLES LEE

**(1) WASHINGTON AND HIS GENERALS OR LEGENDS OF THE AMERICAN REVOLUTION
VOL 1, AUTHOR GEORGE LIPPARD, PG-33**

" The one who held the map was tall and straight shouldered and I knew the figure to be that of the General in chief, as I approached I recognized too, the **Swarthy face of General Charles Lee.**"

**(2) IN HOSTILE RED: A ROMANCE OF THE MONMOUTH CAMPAIGN
AUTHOR JOSEPH ALEXANDER ALTSHELER PG-314**

"Standing in the same circle with Pickering and **Lee, the Captain of the Partisan band**, **with his slight form and Swarthy face,** who was on detail on that faithful night with the Commander in chief?"

GENERAL LIGHTHORSE HENRY LEE

FRANK LESLIES ILLUSTRATED NEWSPAPER

VOL 41-43, MAY13, 1876 PG-162

"The **Ruddy** Virginian Light horse Henry Lee".

General Henry Lee was also the Virginia representative to the U.S Congress. **This Ruddy man was the father of Confederate General Robert E. Lee**. This is the best image that I could get of this guy…you can see the whitening taking place around his mouth. **BLACK CONTINENTAL GENERAL.**

GENERAL BARON VON STEUBEN, PRUSSIAN GERMAN & DRILL MASTER

NATIONAL HISTORIC PARK, PENNSYLVANIA, BASE OF STATUE

This black German, Baron Von Steuben, was hired by the Congress of the United States to come to the 13 Colonies and train the Continental army. This image was taken from the base of a statue in Valley Forge National Park , Pennsylvania. Unless you are Ray Charles you should be able see that this relief depicts Baron Von Steuben, the soldiers and his aide as black men! I suspect that the aide holding his coat is none other than General Benjamin Walker.....also a black man...I shall attempt to slow th image down further to get a good look at the Baron and his aide.

GENERAL BARON VON STEUBEN

As you can see, General Baron Von Steuben and his aide are clearly presented as black men. This image matches the statement of Benjamin Franklin," the Germans are swarthy." **BLACK GERMAN BARON VON STEUBEN.**

115

DARK HUED/BLACK GENERAL PULASKI IS ON THE LEAD HORSE WITH HIS SWARTHY/BLACK POLISH ARMY FOLLOWING WITH SWORDS IN HAND.

STATUE, PATTERSON PARK, BALTIMORE MD

WASHINGTON AND HIS GENERALS OR LEGENDS OF THE AMERICAN REVOLUTION VOL 1, PG-39

"Ha **that gallant band whom comes trooping on**, spurring their stout steeds with wild haunches.....**every SWARTHY hand raising the sword** on high.....**they wear the look of foreigners...**trained to fight in the exterminating wars of Europe. Their leader, **Pulaski,** is tall and proportioned with a **dark hued** (hued=colored) **face.**

The memoirs said that these black men came from Europe, **not Africa**, which is 4,512 miles from Africa. **BLACK POLISH CONTINENTAL GENERAL.**

116

GEORGE WASHINGTON

Are there any memoirs from the 18th century that give an eyewitness description of George Washington? Yes there is but we will have to use multiple memoirs of people that actually knew George Washington. The eyewitness description of George Washington and his French forefather is going to destroy the false memories that you were taught by Academia.

KEY WORDS AND DEFINITIONS

SWARTHY=BLACK

RUDDY=RED

MOOR OR MOHREN=BLACK

BOOK-HUGH WYNNE THE FREE QUAKER, PG-463

"**General Washington has <u>blue eyes</u> and <u>ruddy skin</u>**".

"I began to see the faces plainly, being as I have said not 15 feet away from the window. **Sir William Howe** was dancing with Miss Redman. I was struck as other have been with his likeness to Washington."

Washington resembled Sir William Howe. What did the British Commander in Chief William Howe look like?

THIS IS AN ACCURATE IMAGE OF THE BLACK BRITISH COMMANDER IN CHIEF WILLIAM HOWE.

THE AMERICAN REVOLUTION 100
THE BATTLES PEOPLE AND EVENTS OF THE AMERICAN REVOLUTION, PG-58

"Commander in Chief William Howe was Swarthy, 6ft tall with bad teeth."

This would mean that General George Washington had a Swarthy complexion! I was sitting at Mac Donald's **(my other office)** trying to put the finishing touches on this book and I decided to do an experiment. I counted 15 feet from the window and looked from where I was standing to see if I could see the faces of people approaching the window or sitting in their cars...and I could. I was able to see their faces and the color of their skin perfectly.

"General Washington looks like Colonel Benedict Arnold". What did General Arnold look like? Come and see.

(1) BOOK- HUGH WYNNE THE FREE QUAKER PG-385

"Major Arnold is a **DARK man** and **yet ruddy** with a large nose".

LE GENERAL ARNOLD, DES CHEFS DE L ARMEE, ANGLO AMERICAINE

PUBLISHER, PARIS CHEZ ESNAUTS & RAPILLY, GENGEBACH GERMANY 1778

LIBRARY OF CONGRESS REPRODUCTION# LC-DIG-PGA-10525

COPY FROM THE ORIGINAL ITEM!

This image of Benedict Arnold fits the description given to us by Hugh Wynn. This engraving was completed in France in the year 1780.

DARK=BLACK

SWARTHY=BLACK

RUDDY=RED

GEORGE WASHINGTON.

GENERAL GEORGE WASHINGTON, LIBRARY OF CONGRESS

Based on the eyewitness account given to us by Huge Wynne, a surreal (unusual) image of George Washington begins to emerge. **George Washington was dark, swarthy** and **ruddy** with blue eyes...this is the testimony of the people that knew him personally. Is this it...is this all the evidence that I have? Of course not, I have a greater witness than this...come and see.

STATUE OF GEORGE WASHINGTON	GEORGE WASHINGTON HEAD CROPPED OFF STATUE	GEORGE WASHINGTON CROPPED HEAD LIGHTENED

STATUE OF GEORGE WASHINGTON

ILE DE RE COGNACK MUSEUM FRANCE

This statue of George Washington was found 4,760 miles from America, in the country of France and it depicts him as a black man. **I have broken this statue down in three phases;** the statue of George Washington untouched, the statues head cropped off **and the head of the statue lightened**. On the next page I set the lightened head of George Washington statue next to the image of George Washington found at the library of Congress and......... I was stunned!

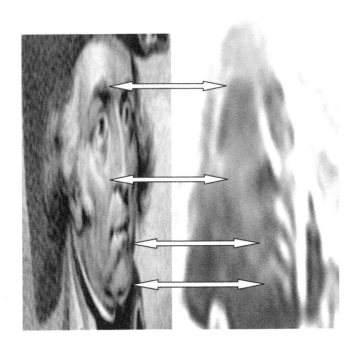

The image on the left is an image of George Washington that is currently housed at the Library of Congress. The face of the statue on the right is from the Ile De Re, Cognack Museum in France. When I set the lightened statue's head beside the image of George Washington's engraved image...it is a perfect match. Based on the memoirs, the Library of Congress image and the statue from France **it appears that we have found the real George Washington!** The memoirs of the people that knew George Washington personally are accurate and very detailed. Let's view the image of George Washington's great, great, great grandfather that is on the base of the statue.

NICHOLAS MARTIAU, ERNEST
COGNACQ MUSEUM

ST. MARTIN DE RE FRANCE

NICOLAS MARTIAU FRENCH/BASQUE

GREAT, GREAT, GREAT GRANDFATHER OF GEORGE WASHINGTON

This is an image of George Washington's black/swarthy great ancestor, the French Huguenot, Nicolas Martiau. This black man came to America in 1620 on the ship Francis Bonaventure and he is depicted as a black man! Nicolas had **a daughter by the name of Elizabeth Martiau,** this black French woman married **Colonel Read (black Brit) a man**

from Britain/Wales. A daughter was born to them by the name of Mildred Martiau, a black woman, who in turn married Colonel Augustus Warner and to them was born the illustrious George Washington.

Benjamin Franklin said," the French are swarthy/black and when he traveled to France he wrote," the Frenchmen in Northern France are swarthy/black."

Thomas Jefferson wrote during the storming of the Bastille in France," I saw 60,000 Frenchmen of all colors storming the Bastille."

These are the facts (nonfiction) as they have been handed down to this generation. **<u>George Washington had French Huguenot Basque blood in him</u>** from his great, great, great grandfather's side of the family. Franklin's mother was a black woman being the offspring of two black Nations; the French black Basque and the black Brit/Welsh.

Professor Boyd Dawkins said," the black Britain's were pushed westward into Wales and Scotland."

This is the reason Washington was described as being swarthy and ruddy, he was a mulatto French/Welsh Prince. Have you ever seen a street fight that started in the street and then it ended up in somebody's front yard? This great argument **(memoirs)** has come forth from the grave and is banging on the front doors of Academia. It is time to examine the black occupation of the 13 colonies.

124

CHAPTER 8:   BLACK BRITISH OCCUPATION

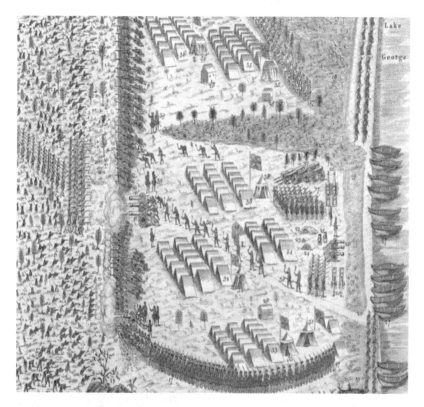

BATTLE OF LAKE GEORGE, 1756 ENGRAVING

ENGRAVER SAMUEL BLODGET 1724, LONDON 1756

The battle of Lake George was an attempt by the British to expel the French from North America. I am not concerned with the particulars of that battle.....my interest lies in the color of the British troops. I have enlarged the image on the next page so that the blackness of the Red coats can be plainly seen. See the next page.

BLACK BRITISH SOLDIERS AT FOX LAKE CROPPED FROM IMAGE ON PG-125

Do you see all of these black British/German soldiers? These images prove that the British/Welsh and the Germans were a black people during the American Revolution.

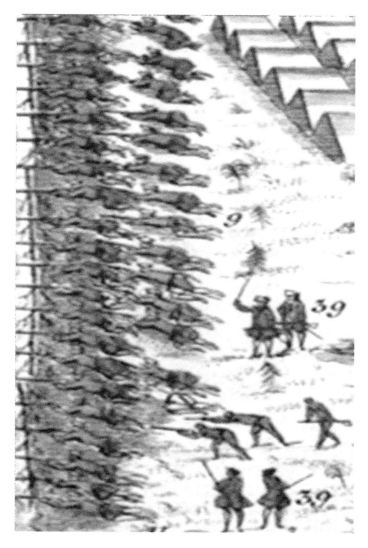

CROPPED FROM IMAGE ON PG-125

As you can see I have slowed the picture down by blowing up parts of the image to make it clear to you that the British/German/Hessian soldiers were black!

BLACK INDIANS, IMAGE CROPPED FROM PG-125

Benjamin Franklin said," all of America is swarthy/black and William Penn said," the Indians are black! What happened to the black Indians? The whites committed genocide against the swarthy American Indians under the pretense of Manifest Destiny. After the **black Indians** were **exterminated**, the **whites assumed their identity** and **took their lands**; this is how the white Indian came into being. Prior to Manifest destiny there was no such thing as a white Indian. Identity theft is not a new concept in the Earth; when the Assyrians deported the 10 tribes they placed Assyrians in Samaria and when the Babylonians deported Judah, Edom took Judah's land and assumed his identity.....to this very day!

HISTORICAL CARICATURE OF THE CHEROKEE NATION

LIBRARY OF CONGRESS

When the whites began the extermination of the American Indian they created this cartoon but what I want to focus on is the color of the American Indian. The Government propaganda at that time depicted the American Indian as a black man and why? This is what they knew to be true in their generation and this is identical in nature to the comment made by Benjamin Franklin," all of America is wholly swarthy/black." This is why I made the statement that **the white Indian is a new concept in the** Earth…during colonial times there was no such thing!

129

PRESIDENT ANDREW JACKSON-FRENCH HUGUENOT BASQUE BLOOD

LITHOGRAPH 1830 LIBRARY OF CONGRESS

This is an original print of **President Andrew Jackson** being depicted as a black Frenchman....along **with the** various **Black Indian Chiefs!** Take a closer look at the picture on the wall behind Jackson....**the Indian is depicted as black**

person and lady Britain is depicted as a white woman! This portrait of Andrew Jackson supports the noise out there that says he was a black man. Our focus today is not on Andrew Jackson but the black American Indian....all of the images from the 18th century depicts the Indian as a man of color. I shall produce another eyewitness...the founder of Pennsylvania...William Penn.

MEMOIRS OF THE PUBLIC AND PRIVATE LIFE OF WILLIAM PENN
PG-140

WILLIAM PENN

"For the natives **(Indians)** I shall consider them in their persons, language, manners, religion and Government. For their persons they are generally tall, straight and well built and of singular proportion. **Their complexion is BLACK**....**like the Gypsies in England!** They grease themselves with bear fat and using no defense against the sun and weather **their skin must be SWARTHY."**

William Penn not only tells us that **the Indians in North America** were black but he tells us that they **are black as the Europeans in England**.....wow! William Penn also gives us the definition of Swarthy....**Penn said," black is Swarthy."** Benjamin Franklin said the same exact thing in 1751.

131

Memoirs of Benjamin Franklin

Benjamin Franklin, William Temple Franklin, William Duane;
Benjamin Franklin Collection (Library of Congress)

BLACK AMERICAN INDIAN

PER THE MEMOIRS OF BENJAMIN FRANKLIN

I took this image from the Memoirs of Benjamin Franklin; it was located in the introduction page. What is the point? Benjamin Franklin was like a news reporter at the scene....he reported the news of his generation accurately, I believe Franklin's report.

The RECONCILIATION between BRITANIA and her daughter AMERICA.

POLITICAL CARTOON 1780, BRITANIA RECONCILES WITH HER DAUGHTER AMERICA

CATALOGUE OF PRINTS AND DRAWINGS BRITISH MUSEUM, BM5989

It should be apparent to you by now that the people of the 18th century drew and depicted the American Indians as they actually knew them....black. **Benjamin Franklin said," America is swarthy,"** it appears that he was not lying.....**Lady America and the American Indians are depicted as black people.** The statue of Liberty used to be called Lady America and was depicted as a black woman! Now that the whites are in power **the black Lady America has become the white statue of liberty.**

BOSTON 1775

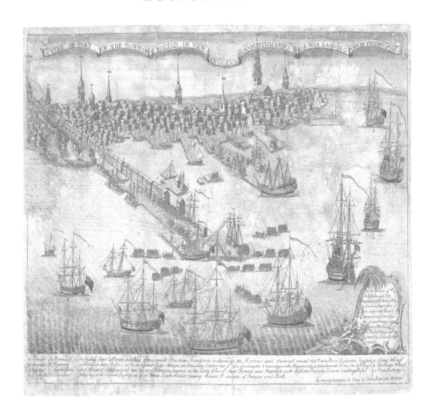

LANDING OF THE BRITISH TROOPS 1775

ENGRAVER, PAUL REVERE

AMERICAN ANTIQUARIAN SOCIETY

This image of the invasion of Boston Harbor by British troops doesn't look like much does it? It looks like a pretty picture with boats floating in a harbor. That is not the case; when you blow the image up... the precious jewels begin to emerge. See the next page!

IMAGE CROPPED FROM PG-134

These images that you are seeing are **the black British/German/Hessian troops (red coats)** as they are disembarking the war ships. I gave you two shots of the same image because I couldn't tell which one was the best shot. I deliberately showed you the ships coming into the Boston Harbor and the black British soldiers disembarking the ships. I wanted to make sure you saw this scene slowed down to its fullest extent. This is what I meant when **I said the Government** sponsored school system has **filled the minds** of the population **with false memories**. These are the true memoires from the past but they will never make it into the Federal funded school system.

These are the Germans that Benjamin Franklin was talking about when he said,'" **why should the Germans** swarm into our settlements? "**They are swarthy/black and can never acquire our complexion** or our customs."

These are the **true memories of** Benjamin **Franklin**. In Benjamin Franklin's generation the Germans were a black swarthy people. The English were white and the Britain's/Welsh were black....it's that simple. If anybody knew what the British/Germans looked like it would've been the famous Paul Revere. The man related his memories in the form of art and he drew what he knew to be true in his generation. I want you to see the Boston massacre from Paul Revere's true memories on the next page! **Come and see.**

THE BOSTON MASSACRE BY PAUL REVERE

ENGRAVING, THE BOSTON MASSACRE 1770

ENGRAVER, PAUL REVERE, LIBRARY OF CONGRESS

Paul Revere completed this engraving of the Boston massacre **3 weeks after the incident.** He painted images of a black British General Preston and black British/German troops. It is a historical fact that the British hired German mercenaries to squash the rebellion in the 13 colonies...this they won't deny. They have a problem admitting that this British army consisted of black Scots, Germans and Welshmen/Britain's! These are Paul Revere's true memories, the only thing that we have been exposed to in the school system are **false memories. False memories are designed** to maintain **the artificial man** (so-called Negro) **or** the **hybrid.** This is one of the most important documents from the colonial era.

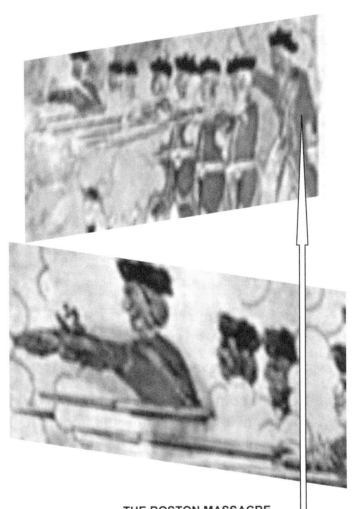

THE BOSTON MASSACRE

IMAGE CROPPED FROM PG-137

This engraving at the Library of Congress is unique; it depicts the British Commander Thomas Preston and his men as black men. Paul Revere was an engraver, silversmith and industrialist...he was also the famous rider who warned the colonists that the

British were coming. In order to warn the colonists that the British were coming Paul Revere had to have seen them...right? **Paul Revere** saw the British and his **true memories** describe a black British army invading Boston. The city of Boston was occupied by 2000 black British/German soldiers and yet....not one of them is depicted in American history...not one! We have the true memories of Paul Revere **(art form)** and Benjamin Franklin **(essay)** stating that the British/German army was black. I want to use the analogy of a dishonest produce vendor. When you go to the market you weigh your fruits and vegetables on a scale and you walk away from the scale with an idea of what your purchase will cost. Once you get to the counter to pay for your produce, the price that the vendor is asking for conflicts with the scale price and so you refuse to pay. If the memories that you were taught don't line up with the memories of the eyewitness, it means the vendor **(school system)** is unjust and you should refuse his narrative. This engraving represents a current event from that generation because it was created 3 weeks after the incident. **The time** frame **(3 weeks after) makes this** one of **the most credible artifacts to survive** the **colonial era**! I have a greater witness than this...**come and see. BLACK OCCUPATION OF BOSTON 7 YEARS.**

BRITISH OCCUPATION OF NEW YORK 1775

BRITISH/ GERMAN HESSIAN SOLDIERS, MARCHING INTO NEW YORK WITH GENERAL HOWE

FRANCAIS-DU FEW TERRIBLE A NOUVELLE YORCK

NEW YORK PUBLIC LIBRARY, IMAGE ID-PSNYPL-PRN-972URL

I want you to pay attention to this great deception in this painting. The British soldiers with the red coats on have their faces painted white but they forgot to paint the faces of the soldiers bringing up the rear, let's move on to the next page.

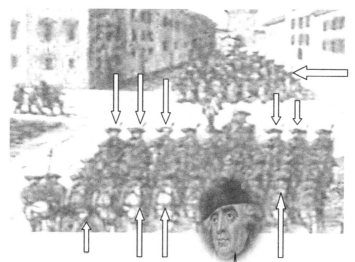

BRITISH GERMAN HESSIAN SOLDIERS MARCHING INTO NEW YORK WITH COMMANDER IN CHIEF WILLIAM BILLY HOWE

IMAGE CROPPED OFF OF PG-140

ARROWS POINTING TO THE ATTEMPT TO WHITEN THE IMAGE!

THE AMERICAN REVOLUTION 100, THE BATTLES PEOPLE AND EVENTS OF THE AMERICAN REVOLUTION, PG-58

"Commander William Howe was Swarthy/black, 6ft tall with bad teeth."

The black German Hessians troops under the command of the black British Commander in Chief (William Howe) invade New York in 1775. The Black British/German/Hessians occupied New York for 6 years. The people who don't want you to know the truth are attempting to paint the black British soldiers faces white. **BLACK OCCUPATION OF NEW YORK 6 YEARS.**

THE BURNING OF NEW YORK

DU FUE TERRIBLE A NOWVELLE YORCK

IMAGE CROPPED FROM PG-140

This image illustrates what the establishment has hidden from the masses over the years. The Government sponsored narrative will be that these were slaves but they cannot prove that...these are the black German Hessian mercenaries that the English hired to put down the revolt in the 13 British colonies. Let us proceed further because this book is full of proof. This information is astonishing...not only did the black Europeans found New York but black Europeans invaded and occupied New York.

IMAGE CROPPED FROM PG-142

This is what the research in The Negro Question Part 6, The 13 Black Colonies proclaimed. In Part 6 I give a timeline in which the black Scottish Colonists arrive into the Colonies. The black Scots began arriving during the reigns of the black Jacobite Scottish Kings; King James 1st of Scotland and England, King Charles the 1st of England , King Charles the 2nd of England and finally King James the 2nd of England. Make no mistake about it, these are the swarthy black Germans that Benjamin Franklin talked about.....**these are not slaves**. I have a greater witness than this...come and see!

SONS OF LIBERTY DESTROY STATUE OF KING GEORGE 3RD

WAR OF INDEPENDENCE, BRITISH LIBRARY # 97

This is the image that you see on the front cover of this book. This is an image of the black British soldiers destroying the statue of King George the 3rd of England, a German King! The images are extremely small, so to see the real jewels that this image possesses, it is necessary to enlarge this image on the next page.

CROPPED FROM PG-144

As you can see....all of these German Hessian soldiers are black. These black men are black German mercenaries.....they are not former slaves. These black colonists include; Germans, Swedes, Dutch, Norwegians, Bohemians, Prussians, French, Brits, Scots and Irish. **The Government sponsored narrative is beginning to come apart at the seam!** <u>Where did all of these free black citizens of New York come from?</u> Let's read a passage from the 13 colonies written by Helen Ainslie on the next page.

"This colony **(New York in 1664)** then numbered some 7,000 Dutch; this is besides the real Dutch, Prussians Bohemians, French, Swedes, Norwegians, Scots, Welsh, Irish and 5000 English. What color were these people?

BENJAMIN FRANKLIN

AMERICA AS A LAND OF OPPORTUNITY

Benjamin Franklin said," **the Swedes, French and Germans were swarthy.** German people include; Prussians, Bohemians, Dutch and Swedes.

According to Benjamin Franklins doubling theory **(every 25 years a population should double)** by the year 1764....there would be 112,000 black Dutchman and Germans in New York City. The Scotch/ Irish and the Welsh/Wales or Britain's were black also. What did Helen Ainslie mean when she said, "7000 Dutch besides the real Dutch? Since the Dutch were the original founders of New York it was assumed that all the blacks in the city were Dutch....interesting right? **This is why the citizens in this photo are black**; they are the seed of the original founders of New York! **If you are one of the guys you will know what this means**; the same thing happened when the seed of Ham and the seed of Shem was herded on ships and brought to North America. Since both groups were black they were called Africans and this confusion continues until this very day...among Africans, black Americans and the entire World.

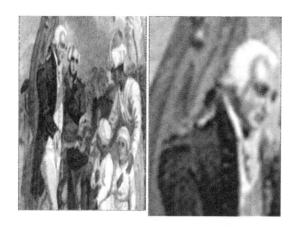

GENERAL LORD CHARLES CORNWALLIS

BOOK- THE HISTORY OF THE WAR FROM THE COMMENCEMENT OF THE FRENCH REVOLUTION TO THE PRESENT TIME, VOLUME 1

AUTHOR, HEWSON CLARK, PUBLISHED 1816

General Cornwallis (his aide) surrendered **8000 black British/German/Hessian troops** to a swarthy/ruddy George Washington at Yorktown. The white images printed in the books sanctioned by the Texas State school board, **as it relates to Colonial history**, is nothing but the unchecked imagination of an evil mind. The tissue that you use to wipe your nose with has more value than the images printed in those books. **BLACK OCCUPATION OF NEW YORK 6 YEARS.**

View of The ATTACK on BUNKER'S HILL, with the Burning of CHARLES TOWN, June 17, 1775.

ATTACK ON BUNKER HILL & THE BURNING OF CHARLESTON
1775 WIKEPEDIA ENCYCLOPEDIA

The British attacked Charleston in 1775 but couldn't overcome the city. In the year 1780 British General Cornwallis, along with the black German Hessian troops, invade and occupy Charleston Massachusetts until the year 1782. **BLACK OCCUPATION OF CHARLESTON 2 and ½ YEARS.**

IMAGE CROPPED FROM PG-148

This is an authentic image of the black British/German troops as they are entering and unloading in Charleston Harbor. This history that you are reading has been hidden from the entire World...including your preacher! It is written," that if it were possible, they would fool the very elect." **BLACK OCCUPATION OF MASSACHUSSETS, 7 YEARS.**

BATTLE OF GREEN SPRING VIRGINIA 1781

MAP, JEAN NICOLAS DESANDROUINS, 18TH CENT

On the left side of this map we have the British/German army being led by the black British General Cornwallis. On the right side of the map the Continental army is being led by General Marquis Lafayette and the black Continental General Wayne. The black Continental soldiers are Scotch/Irish, Welsh, French, Dutch and French.

150

BLACK OFFICERS AT BRANDYWINE

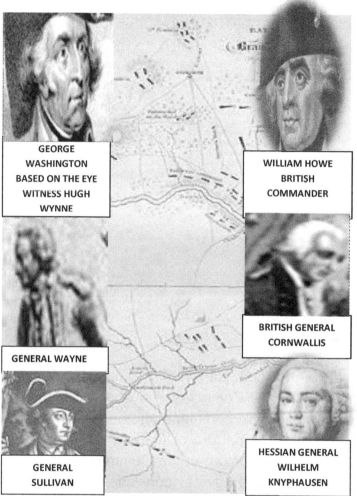

GEORGE WASHINGTON BASED ON THE EYE WITNESS HUGH WYNNE

WILLIAM HOWE BRITISH COMMANDER

GENERAL WAYNE

BRITISH GENERAL CORNWALLIS

GENERAL SULLIVAN

HESSIAN GENERAL WILHELM KNYPHAUSEN

On the left side of this map are the continental officers under General Washington at Brandywine. On the right side of the map are the officers that fought under Commander William Howe. The British occupied Philadelphia from September 1778 to June 1778....exactly 10 months. **BLACK OCCUPATION OF BRANDYWINE 10 MONTHS.**

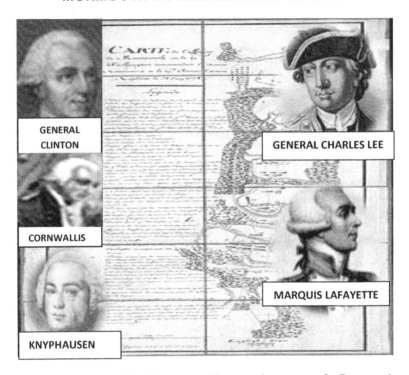

I have provided you with an image of General Henry Clinton, the Commander in Chief of the British army. Clinton took command of the British armed forces after the departure of General William Howe. Based on the Caricature of the Commander in Chief, Sir Henry Clinton, I have to conclude that he was a black man and....he also came from the highlands of Scotland.

SIEGE OF SAVANNAH GEORGIA

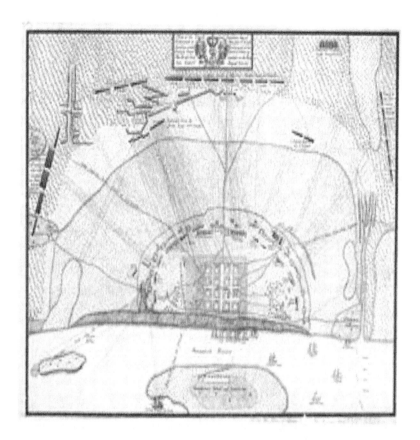

Savannah Georgia was captured by a black British Lieutenant by the name of Lt. Colonel Archibald Campbell. Before I deal with the taking of Savannah Georgia by this black Scotch/Irish General, let's take a look at his pedigree. This Archibald Campbell was a black Scot from the Highlands of Scotland and Professor Boyd Dawkins gives great insight as to the color of the Highlanders.

"The English invaded Britain in 449 and carved out the Kingdom Northumberland. The English **pushed** the black Britain's Westward into Wales, Cumberland, Westmoreland, **Highlands of Scotland, Cornwall** and Devon.

HADRIAN'S WALL- BUILT TO KEEP THE WHITE BARBARIANS OUT OF BRITAIN, LONG BEFORE THE NAME WAS CHANGED TO WALES.

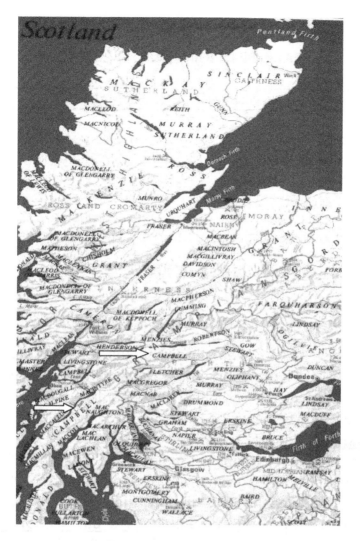

The Campbell clans were black Britain's that were pushed into the Highlands of Scotland. I have a greater witness than this map. See the ships manifest on the next page. This clan name can be found all over the Caribbean.

SHIPS MANIFEST, THE VETERAN 1745

PLACE OF ORIGINATION, LIVERPOOL

FIRST	LAST NAME	AGE	REMARKS
ROBERT	ADAM	18	BROWN SMOOTH FACE
WILLIAM	BELL	46	BLACK, CURLED HAIR
DOUGALL	CAMPBELL	18	BROWN COMPLEXION
ALEXANDER	CATTANACH	17	BLACK RUDDY
DOUGALL	CAMPBELL	18	BROWN, RUDDY
ALEXANDER	CAMPBELL	18	BROWN, POCK PITTED

JACOBITE GLEANINGS FROM STATE MANUSCRIPTS

PGS 37-48

AUTHOR J.MACBETH FORBES, HARVARD COLLEGE LIBRARY

This is an eyewitness account of **the black** Jacobite **(Hebrew Israelites)** Noblemen, Princes and captured soldiers as they are boarding the Prison ships to be shipped into the 13 colonies. **The Campbell's are described as brown and** ruddy **people;** these Campbell's match the description of the Highlanders given by Professor Dawkins. What does this mean? **This means that racist Georgia was captured and occupied by a black Scottish Highlander.....Lt. Archibald Campbell... along with his black German Hessian soldiers.** The black Hessians fought off the continental army led by General Benjamin Lincoln and Comte de Estaing. **During the siege of Savannah 4000 free black Haitian's** fought on the side of the American Colonists.

156

LED BY COLONEL CAMPBELL, THE BLACK BRIT/GERMAN TROOPS

GENERAL COMTE ESTANG

BLACK BRITISH GERMAN TROOPS

FREE HAITIAN TROOPS

FREE CONTINENTAL TROOPS

This is the true history of the occupation and siege of Savannah Georgia. The black British/German/ Hessian invasion force fought off the black French and black Haitian forces. There were 4 black armies present in Georgia. **Shout this** on the top of Stone Mountain Georgia!! **BLACK OCCUPATION OF SAVANNAH GEORGIA 4 YEARS.**

AQUIDNECK RHODE ISLAND 1778

GENERAL JOHN SULLIVAN

GENERAL CLINTON

GEN. COMTE ESTANG

MEMOIRS OF HENRY ARMITT BROWN

TOGETHER WITH 4 HISTORICAL ORATIONS PG-330

JOHN SULLIVAN- NEW HAMPSHIRE LIBRARY AND LIBRARY OF CONGRESS

"Swarthy John Sullivan a little headstrong but brave as a lion."

The General of record for the Continental army was General John Sullivan from New Hampshire. The eyewitness description of him makes him a black man but get this... he led an army of blacks, whites and black Indians. The siege of Rhode Island took place in August of 1778 and lasted 21 days before the American Continental forces departed. **The black British German/Hessians invaded and occupied Rhode Island for 3 long years.** The British Generals of Record was General Clinton and **General Richard Prescott. BLACK OCCUPATION OF RHODE ISLAND 3 YEARS.**

BATTLE OF WHITE MARSH PHILADELPHIA 1777

LIBRARY OF CONGRESS, GEOGRAPHY AND MAP DIVISION

AUTHOR, JOHANN MARTIN WILL, AUGSBURG GERMANY 1777

The British fielded an army at the battle of White Marsh and the General of record for the British was none other than General Cornwallis. Cornwallis was a black British General who came from Cornwall...this is one of the regions in Scotland that Professor Boyd Dawkins said that the black Britain's were pushed into. The ledger gives the number and the name of the horse rider as General Cornwallis. I blew the image up on the next page.

PART OF THE FACE HAS BEEN WHITENED TO ATTEMPT TO
HIDE THE BLACKNESS OF CORNWALLIS.

GENERAL CORNWALLIS IMAGE CROPPED FROM PG-160

According to the legend on page 160, the man leading the infantry **(#1)** at White Marsh Philadelphia was none other than General Cornwallis. If you look closely at Cornwallis face, you can see someone attempted to whiten the image. Thank God for the haters of this World....you need haters...if the haters had never tried to whiten Cornwallis face we never would have known he was black!

This image was cropped off from the original on page 160, I have enlarged it to the best of my abilities. Take a real close look at these black German/Hessian artilliary men that are fighting under the British flag. I placed two shots of the same image on this page in hopes that you are able to see the black German grenadiers. **BLACK OCCUPATION OF PHILADELPHIA 1 YEAR.**

BENJAMIN FRANKLIN

ESSAY: AMERICA AS A LAND OF OPPORTUNITY
1751

"And **since Detachments of English from Britain** sent to America, will have their Places at Home so soon supply'd and increase so largely here; **why should the Palatine Boors [Germans] be suffered to swarm into our Settlements,** and by herding together establish their Language and Manners to the Exclusion of ours? Why should Pennsylvania, founded by the English, become a Colony of Aliens, **who will shortly be so numerous as to Germanize us** instead of our Anglifying them, and will never adopt our Language or Customs, **any more than they can acquire our Complexion?**

Let's see how many black Germans and Scots herded into the colonies.

WHAT POLITENESS DEMANDED

ETHNIC OMMISIONS IN BENJAMIN FRANKLIN'S
AUTOBIOGRAPHY

MARC L HARRIS, PENN STATE UNIVERSITY

"It is well-documented that both Philadelphia and Pennsylvania were home to a large and diverse non-British population during the eighteenth century. When Franklin arrived in the city in 1723, its population of about 5,000 already included large numbers of <u>Germans</u> and <u>Scotch-Irish</u> in addition to its **English** and **Welsh** (Welsh=black Britain's) inhabitants. **Over the following thirty years**, while Franklin became first a prominent printer and then a professional public figure and noted natural philosopher, the city was inundated by immigrants. **Some 40,000 black German-speakers landed at Philadelphia** in the period and **a further 30,000 black Scotch-Irish** migrants entered Pennsylvania. There were over 80,000 blacks entering Philadelphia within 30 years of Benjamin Franklin's arrival. The Welsh/Wales are the original black Britain's that were pushed into Wales by the invading whites in the year 449 A.D. The 40,000 black Germans are a mixture of black French Huguenots and black Germans. The black Huguenots migrated to **Germany, Ireland and Wales,** following the reversal of the edict of Nantes by **King Louis XIV**, better known as **the Sun King**. When you put the Germans and French in the same room you couldn't tell them apart. When the census was taken the French totals were added to the black German totals….unknowingly. All of this will become clearer by the time you are finishing reading this book. **BLACK BRITISH/GERMAN OCCUPATION OF PHILADELPHIA 1 YEAR.**

THE BLACK ARMIES OF THE AMERICAN REVOLUTION

BLACK BRITISH/GERMAN SOLDIERS   BLACK POLISH ARMY, PULASKI

BLACK FRENCH HUGUENOT SOLDIER   BLACK HAITIAN SOLDIERS

BLACK CONTINENTAL SOLDIERS;
SCOTCH/IRISH AND WELSH   BLACK AMERICAN INDIAN

BEHOLD THE MOHREN/BLACK SOLDIERS

CHAPTER 9: THE ORIGINAL BLACK COLONISTS

So far every army that fought in the Revolutionary war was black but I asked myself this question.....who were the loyalists who fought on the side of the British and what color were they? **By the time I am finished with this chapter you will see that the Loyalist Generals, Captains and Leutenants were black men!** Below is a list of black Scottish Highlander Loyalist who fought on the side of the colonists.....but take note these were free black Majors, Brigadier Generals, Lieutenants and Captains and I shall prove that by the evidence that is available.

CONTINENTAL LOYALISTS ARMY OFFICERS

MAJOR ADAM MCDONALD 1ST CAROLINA REGIMENT

MAJOR DANIEL MCDONALD 3RD NEW JERSEY REGIMENT

CAPTAIN JOHN MCDONALD 6TH PENNSYLVANIA BATTALION

CAPTAIN JAMES MCDONALD 1ST CAROLINA REGIMENT

LIETUTENANT WILLIAM MCDONALD 3RD NJ REGIMENT

LIEUTENANT BARNEY MCDONALD 4TH VIRGINIA REGIMENT

LIEUTENANT WILLIAM MCDONALD 4TH GEORGIA REGIMENT

LIEUTENANT MICHAEL MCDONALD BRITISH NAVY

MAJOR RICHARD MCDONALD 1ST BATTALION NJ REGIMENT

CAPTAIN LEWIS MCDONALD JR 2ND REGIMENT NEW YORK

WHERE DID THE MCDONALD'S COME FROM?

This is a list of Continental Loyalist officers that fought against the English during the great American rebellion or the American revolutionary war. If you look at the last names on this list, they are all MacDonald's and Scottish Highlanders. I have inserted a ships manifest from the Jacobite rebellions that describe the Mc Donald highlanders **(colonists)** as they are boarding the rebellion ships. Before I show you the ships manifest, which gives an accurate description of the Mc Donald men, I want to refresh your memory concerning the skin color of the Highlanders.

PROF. BOYD DAWKINS 1837-1929

BRITISH GEOLOGIST, ARCHAEOLOGIST, ESSAY; OUR EARLIEST
ANCESTORS PAGE 96 & 97

"In the year **449 A.D** certain Englishmen came from North Germany and the Southern shores of the Baltic Sea and pushed the Britain's westward. By the year 607 A.D the English had pushed the Britain's westward as far as Chester. **"The English** carved out **Yorkshire, Chester and Southern Lancashire forming the Kingdom of Northumbria."**

Professor Boyd Dawkins is giving the location of the whites that invaded Britain. Professor Boyd Dawkins continued on the next page.

Professor Boyd Dawkins cont'd

"The inhabitants of Britain belong to very different races; Britain was inhabited by the black **Basque** from ancient times and **they called themselves Roman citizens**. <u>In their books</u> they were called the Britain's or Welsh; <u>there are two type of Welsh, one is</u> **dark and 5 feet 4 inches** <u>and the other is</u> **tall and round headed**. "**The English pushed the Dark Welsh/Britain Westward into <u>Wales,</u>** Cumberland, Westmoreland, **<u>Highlands of Scotland,</u>** Cornwall and Devon."

<u>Professor Boyd Dawkins is giving the location of the blacks in Wales</u>. See the spreadsheet below that lists some of the black Scots and the new black European colonists that are being sent into the colonies.

NEW BLACK COLONISTS BEING SENT TO THE 13 COLONIES

FIRST	LAST NAME	AGE		REMARKS
ANGUS	MCINTOSH	26		BLACK
PETER	MCINTOSH	34		BROWN
JAMES	MCPHEARSON	22		BLACK
ALEXANDER	MCLEOD	18	XXXXXXX	BROWN
CHARLES	MORGAN	18		BROWN
DONALD	MCGILLIS	18		BLACK
ALLEN	MCDOUGALL	26		BLACK
ANGUS	**MCDONALD**	**60**		**BLACK**

CONVICT SHIP; THE VETERAN, POLITICAL PRISONERS CONTINUED

These black men on these ships manifest will form the Continental army during the American Revolution.

"Land was granted to **Angus Mc Donald** on the east side of the Kinderhook River. **During the Jacobite rising of 1745, McDonald** fought as a lieutenant under the command of Charles Edward Stuart in the Battle of Culloden, after which he was "attainted of treason." He fled Scotland, departing from Inverness for the colony of Virginia in 1746 at the age of 18. Following his arrival in Virginia, McDonald worked as a merchant in Falmouth for two or three years. In 1765 McDonald returned to military service when he was commissioned by Thomas Fairfax, 6th Lord Fairfax of Cameron, as a major in command of the Frederick County militia. Lord Fairfax also appointed McDonald as an attorney and land agent for his Northern Neck Proprietary. Governor John Murray, 4th Earl of Dunmore, commissioned McDonald in 1774 as a ranking military officer of an expedition. The expedition was formed to organize and recruit settlers **(black Scotch/Irish)** west of **the Allegheny Mountains**. The recruit's mission was to defend settlements from Native American attacks. McDonald completed the expedition, which met its goal of temporarily relieving western Virginia frontier settlements from attack.

THESE ARE THE ORIGINAL BLACK COLONIST'S

FIRST	LAST NAME	AGE		REMARKS
GEORGE	SAMUEL	18		BROWN
JAMES	DONALD	20		BROWN
ANDREW	MATTHEW	20		DARK COMPLEXION
WILLIAM	JACKSON	19		BROWN LUSTY
DONALD	**MCDONALD**	**58**		**SWARTHY**
ANGUS	**MACDONALD**	**60**		**BLACK MAN**
WILLIAM	ROSS	36	XXXXXXX	RUDDY
DUNCAN	CAMPBELL	16		DARK COMPLEXION
JOHN	CUNNINGHAM	32		BLACK, STURDY

SHIPS MANIFEST LOCATION

JACOBITE GLEANINGS PAGE 37-41

What are you really looking at? <u>You are looking at an accurate description of the black colonists and the black continental army.</u> These black Jacobites were deported into the 13 British colonies in 1715 and 1745. These men and their offspring filled the ranks of the Continental army during the American Revolution, **this is indisputable!**

ARTICLE HISTORY OF THE CLAN DONALD, HENRY JAMES LEE

At the time of the outbreak of the Revolution there was **a large settlement of Scottish colonists at Cross Creek, in North Carolina.** They brought with them to the new country, the sturdy senitiments of the Covenanters, but loyalty was an inherent principle in their character, **and when <u>Donald McDonald</u>** called upon his countrymen to remember their oath of allegiance to the Crown, they, at first followed him to oppose the patriot army. As the rebellion assumed the phase of resistance to oppression and redress of wrongs, **the black Highlanders switched allegiance and fought on the Continental side.**

What does the writer mean...they fought on the side of the **Covenanters?** The only people to keep the covenant was the Hebrew Israelites/Jacobites, these are the black men listed on the spreadsheet on pages 168 and170. **Donald McDonald (a Jacobite) was commissioned a Brigadier General of the British Forces** by Lord Dunmore, and gathered more than one **thousand black Scots** around him. According to the ships manifest he was a Swarthy black man! He had fought for Prince Charles Edward at Culloden and had great influence over his colonist countrymen. **Also at Cross Creek, lived Flora MacDonald,** the heroine of the Prince's wanderings and escape, and she used all her influence to rally the Scots to General McDonald's standard. **The original black colonists of the 13 British colonies have been deleted from real colonial history.** I was painting a black floor with red paint one day and it occurred to me that even though the red paint was showing....the black paint was still beneath the red paint, you just couldn't see it. **Once in a while the top paint peels or chips** and you can see the original color of the paint beneath it. **The white paint is beginning to peel off of real colonial history** and **we are beginning to see the blackness of the American Revolution** that has been **hidden beneath the white paint.** Together we are chipping the paint off of colonial and World history and together we shall prevail! The word **Mc Donald means** the son of Donald **and there is a black Donald (Mc Donald)** being held without bond in a string of killings in Tampa Florida. Through the reckless reporting of the news by the media, along with the news conference that the Mayor and police chief gave, how on Earth can this black man receive a fair trial?

The **evidence** has **not** been **produced**, the man has **not confessed** to the murders, the ballistics have not come back and yet during this press conference the police chief said," **this is the guy.**" Do you want to hear something equally confusing? They have already given the reward money to the Mc Donald's manager and this man has not been convicted yet. Is this man a descendant of the black British Commander in Chief William Howe and is he related to the famous Mc Donald's from the highlands of Scotland? Based on my knowledge of real colonial history...I think he is. See Flora Mc Donald on the next page.

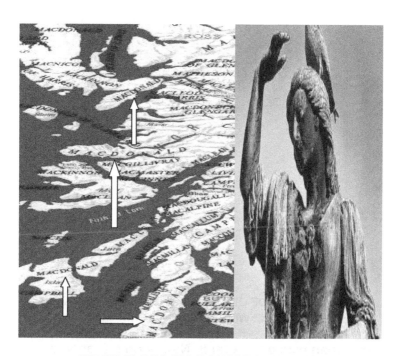

IMAGE FLORA MC DONALD WIKEPEDIA

INVERNESS CASTLE, UK

Clearly these are the Highlands of Scotland....Professor Boyd Dawkins said that the black Britain's were pushed westward into the Highlands of Scotland. This is why the clown, Ronald Mc Donald is represented with an afro, big feet and a big nose. It is subliminal...the people that are in power know that the real McDonald was a black man, so what do they do? They create a clown called Ronald Mc Donald and turn him into a buffoon. The supposition (belief) is that black people have big feet, big noses and huge afros....subliminal. See the next page.

173

MARSHALL JACQUES
MACDONALD

STATUE ON THE SIDE OF THE LOUVRE ON RUE DE RIVOLI,
PARIS & THE WIKEPEDIA ENCYCLOPEDIA

This man was a general in Napoleon's French army, a **relative of Flora Macdonald** and he is depicted just like the other Macdonald's....black! Throughout this time, MacDonald worked closely with Tsar Alexander, who asked MacDonald to personally draw the map of demarcation **(mark a boundary)** for the armistice. A brief period of negotiation resulted in the Treaty of Fontainebleau, a document that ended Napoleon's rule as Emperor. <u>**MacDonald was one of only 6 signatories to the document,**</u> which also included Napoleon's faithful aide, Armand de Caulain Court. **Where can this black history be found?** It can only be found here, in the Negro Question book series. You will not be exposed to this in the Government sponsored school system or the Churches.

BLACK RHODE ISLAND REGIMENT-BROWN UNIVERSITY

The so-called scholars can't deny the blackness of the Rhode Island regiment so they have to roll out the party line. The party line is this; the black Rhode Island regiment consisted of former slaves or African Americans. There is one problem with the party line; we have **in our possession** a document that gives a physical **(ships manifest pgs 168-170) description of black Europeans** flooding into the colonies. I also have **in my possession** a **book (pg-14)** that was written **by** former English secret service agent **John Macky,** in which he **describes the Scottish and British nobles as black men.** I have the testimony of 8 white scholars (chpt-1) that testify to the existence of black European Nations. The Government sponsored school system is guilty of fraud and deceit and that is being polite. The false memories taught by this institution help to perpetuate the ideology of white supremacy in the Earth. The Declaration of Independence states that all men are created equal; that is what I believe and that is what I teach!

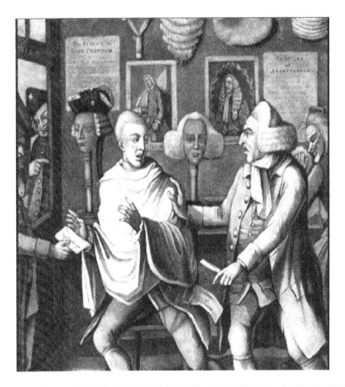

PATRIOTIC BARBER, BRITISH MUSEUM & BROWN UNIVERSITY

This has to be one of the most compelling images that I have ever seen that proves the blackness of the 13 colonies. This image proves that the black colonists owned businesses and were involved in commerce. This scene involves a black British/German young man that went to get a haircut but once the black **Colonist** (black Scot) barber found out that he was a British/German soldier.....he refused him service....but I was taught that blacks only existed in Africa...hmmmn. Take a closer look at **the black manikins** and the young **black German/Britain** fleeing the barbershop on the next few pages.

176

IMAGE CROPPED OFF OF PG-176

These black British colonists were making black images as early as the 17th century. Corporations in America didn't start selling black dolls until 1910…two hundred years later. The **black man is a Nation builder,** if you don't believe me all you have to do is **look at the 54 Nations** that are still standing **in Africa**. The school system is preparing black children to be laborers form the moment they have the ability to reason. You can never make it in America working for someone else; the only one who benefits from your labor is the owner of the business. If you have a business in mind but you just don't know how to get it up and running, this is what you do. You infiltrate your desired industry by taking a job and instead of goofing off on the job; take notes on how they run the business. While you are taking notes, start saving your start up money **(cut out the bank)** and when the time is right you open up the same business.

IMAGE CROPPED FROM PG-176

You are probably surprised that this young German/ Britain is being depicted as a young black man but why? Benjamin Franklin in his essay; America as a land of opportunity 1751 stated," the Germans are **swarthy."** I have an arrow pointing to the white paint splashed on the image; this is what I call cooking the books.

arliest known view of Fraunces Tavern is believed t
the building as it was altered following a fire in
From Valentine's Manual for 1854

BOOK-THE HISTORY OF NEW YORK

MARY LOUISE BOOTH PG-35, 573

BLACK SAM'S TAVERN

General George Washington had his head quarters in a tavern, in New York City, called black Sam's tavern. The reason it was called black Sam's tavern is because **the owner Sam was Swarthy/black**. The tavern was located on the corner of Pearl, then Queen and broad. During the Revolutionary war Fraunces (**Frances)** was referred to as black Sam's. You must not forget that the French were swarthy at this time. George Washington didn't have a problem hanging out in Frances because he was descended from the French on his great, great, great grandfather's side, Nicholas Martinau.

179

**LADY AMERICA BRITAIN POLITICAL CARTOON 1780
JAMES GILRAY**

This image is called the reconciliation between Britannia and her daughter America. The cartoon imagery is misleading because the Britain's/Welsh were black from ancient times. I have no problem with the representation of black America because it matches the eyewitness account of Benjamin Franklin. In the future, **the black statue** of **Lady America** magically **transforms into** the **white statue of Liberty.**

AMERICA DEPICTED AS A BLACK WOMAN

CARTOON PRINTS BRITAIN & LIBRARY OF CONGRESS

This print and others depict America as a black Country.....the female representative that depicts Britain as a white nation is a bold face lie. The only reason that I am focused on the color of America is because this is what **Benjamin Franklin said," all America is swarthy/black.** Who founded America? The black Scotch/Irish and the black Britain's founded America. When the black European colonists arrived in America the black Indian was already in the land. This image of the black lady America **should be represented with black colonists on bent knees**...not white colonists. This imagery of white colonists on bent knees is an attempt to teach false memories through art. That is why Hollywood, the History channel and Museums exist in the United States; they create false memories through fake art.

181

THE PARIS PEACE TREATY 1783

PRESIDENT HENRY LAURENS, FRENCH HUGUENOT

BOSTON MAGAZINE 1784, JOHN NORMAN

THE HANGING OF THOMAS JEREMIAH, A FREE BLACK MAN'S
ENCOUNTER WITH LIBERTY PG-21

"**Elkanah Watson**, a young American Merchant who **met Henry Laurens in France in 1782** remembered him as a pleasant and facetious gentleman of **SWARTHY complexion**, medium size and slender form." **BLACK CONTINENTAL PRESIDENT.**

This black Frenchman was the President of the Continental Congress and he was one of the signees of the articles of Confederation. **This black former President of the Continental Congress** was also sent to London to negotiate a peace treaty between the 13 Colonies and the United Kingdom. <u>Henry Laurens</u> was sent along with Benjamin Franklin, **John Jay (French Huguenot)** and **John Adams (French Huguenot)**

AUTHOR ELKANAH WATSON

PRESIDENT HENRY LAURENS OF CONGRESS

MEN AND TIMES OF THE REVOLUTION: OR MEMOIRS OF ELKANAH WATSON PGS- 138 & 139

"Henry Laurens **(black French Huguenot)** was formerly **President of Congress and was appointed ambassador to Holland.** He was a citizen of South Carolina, a man of great wealth and position. **He had <u>a swarthy complexion,</u>** medium size and slender form. I was set off with Mr. Lauren who was in my vicinity."

In today's language he is saying," Mr. Lauren was in my neighborhood and we started walking together". **Mr. Laurens was Swarthy/black and he was a French Huguenot....**this validates the writings of **Benjamin Franklin when he said," the French are swarthy."** Examine the wording of the letter written by General George Washington to President Lauren on the next page.

183

"However on July 11th **a letter was received from General George Washington**.....immediately upon its receipt it began to be read by Charles Thompson then Secretary of Congress who began to read **the letter," Which was addressed to his Excellency Henry Laurens** and to others....the members of the Congress."

I want to emphasize that President Henry Lauren and his son General Lauren were black British colonists and yet they were of French descent. I wrote the Negro Question Part 6-The 13 Black Colonies and I said that the black Scots founded the 13 colonies but I have to be honest with you, **the blackness that has been concealed under the white paint is astonishing!**

BENJAMIN FRANKLIN 1751

"The French are Swarthy."

PRESIDENT JOHN JAY, FRENCH HUGUENOT

John Jay, one of the signatories of the Treaty of Paris, was the President of the Continental Congress in **the year 1778.** He was a **Swarthy/black** Frenchmen! He later became the first Chief Justice in the 13 Colonies. The date, **1778** is 27 years from the date **(1751)** that Benjamin Franklin said the French were black....this is not enough time for skin color to change from black to white.

PRESIDENT E. BOUDINOT, FRENCH HUGUENOT

Elias Boudinot, a **Swarthy/black** Frenchmen became President of the Continental Congress in the year 1782. This black Frenchmen was President during the final years of the American Revolution and he was descended from the De La Tremblade family in France. The date, **1782** is 31 years from the date **(1751)** that Benjamin Franklin said the French were black....**this is not enough time for skin color to change from black to white.** I have an image of the members of the 2nd Continental Congress......11 of the signees were black Scots.....5 of the signees were black Welsh/Brits, 1 Swede and 2 Irish. **See the next page.**

JOHN BULL DECLARATION OF INDEPENDENCE COIN

LIBRARY OF CONGRESS & WIKEPEDIA

Ten years after the Declaration of Independence was adopted, **John Trumbull <u>traveled the country in a carriage seeking out all the men</u>** who signed the document. <u>**He wanted to paint their likenesses**</u> as part of a monumental work depicting the nation's founding moment. This means the man was an eyewitness to the skin color of the delegates...he saw them face to face. He carried a small painting, protected by a special case, to which he would add each portrait as he found each member of the revolutionary Congress.

LOOK UP ANY OF THE NUMBERED INDIVIDUALS ON THIS MEDAL AND THEN LOCATE THE NAME ON THE KEY BELOW. THE PARAGRAPH BELOW THE KEY WILL LET YOU KNOW FROM WHAT RACE THESE MEN DESCENDED. BASED ON THIS INFORMATION YOU WILL BE ABLE TO DETERMINE EACH MANS TRUE COLOR

2ND CONTINENTAL CONGRESS, ARTIST, JOHN TRUMBULL 1776

rthe, Virginia	13. Arthur Middleton, South Carolina	25. George Clymer, Pennsylvania	37. John Witherspoon, N
/hipple, New Hampshire	14. Thomas Heyward, Jr., South Carolina	26. William Hooper, North Carolina	38. Samuel Huntington,
Jett, New Hampshire	15. Charles Carroll, Maryland	27. Joseph Hewes, North Carolina	39. William Williams, C
Jarrison, Virginia	16. George Walton, Georgia	28. James Willson, Pennsylvania	40. Oliver Wolcott, Con
nch, South Carolina	17. Robert Morris, Pennsylvania	29. Francis Hopkinson, New Jersey	41. John Hancock, Massa
2nry Lee, Virginia	*18. Thomas Willing, Pennsylvania	30. John Adams, Massachusetts	*42. Charles Thomson, S
ams, Massachusetts	19. Benjamin Rush, Pennsylvania	31. Roger Sherman, Connecticut	Pennsylvania
nton, New York	20. Elbridge Gerry, Massachusetts	*32. Robert R. Livingston, New York	43. George Read, Delawa
1ca, Maryland	21. Robert Treat Paine, Massachusetts	33. Thomas Jefferson, Virginia	*44. John Dickinson, Pen
ase, Maryland	22. Abraham Clark, New Jersey	34. Benjamin Franklin, Pennsylvania	45. Edward Rutledge, So
tis, New York	23. Stephen Hopkins, Rhode Island	35. Richard Stockton, New Jersey	46. Thomas McKean, De
loyd, New York	24. William Ellery, Rhode Island	36. Francis Lewis, New York	47. Philip Livingston, N

: 56 signers of the Declaration of Independence. The painting portrays only 47. The 5 men whose names are starred were not signers. The portraits of the fo
i the painting.

ston, New Hampshire	George Taylor, Pennsylvania	Thomas Nelson, Jr., Virginia	Button Gwinnett, Georg
v Jersey	George Ross, Pennsylvania	Francis Lightfoot Lee, Virginia	Lyman Hall, Georgia
'ennsylvania	Caesar Rodney, Delaware	Carter Braxton, Virginia	
'ennsylvania	Thomas Stone, Maryland	John Penn, North Carolina	

The black Scotch/Irish signees; William Hooper-NC, Phillip Livingston-NC, Thomas Mckean-PA, Edward Rutledge-SC, James Smith-PA, James Wilson- PA, John Witherspoon-NJ. **The black Welsh signees; Thomas Jefferson-VA**, Frances Lewis-NY, William Williams-CN, George Reed, number 43 of Irish British descent.

BLACK SCOTS, BRITS, IRISH AND WELSH DELEGATES.

IMAGE CROPPED FROM PG-186

I have numbered the black delegates that are of Welsh, Scottish, Irish and Swedish descent. If one were to travel into the past to look at the participants in the 2nd Continental Congress one would find among the signees; 29 English, **12 black Scotts, 3 black Irish, 2 black French, 2 black Welsh and 1black Dutchman.** Thomas Jefferson is delegate number 33 and guess what.....**Jefferson was a descendant of Wales/Britain and a** ruddy (red) **man.**

THOMAS JEFFERSON

JOHNSONS UNIVERSAL CYCLOPEDIA, VOL 3, PG-757

"**Mr. Jefferson** was tall, well formed, straight and uncommonly strong. **He had sandy hair,** a ruddy complexion and a tranquil benevolent expression."

In Hebrew ruddy means red, Jefferson was either light skinned or a redbone. We see people that fit this description every day on the block (neighborhood).

HUGH WYNN

(1) BOOK- IMAGE, HUGH WYNN,
THE FREE QUAKER, PG-24

(2) BOOK,COLONEL HUGH WYNN
BY SILAS WEIR MITCHELL PG-125

"We all rose as he drew near, my mother saying in my ear as he approached; "now Hugh, it is Arthur Wynn, now Hugh take care." **This newly found cousin was like all of us** (Wynn family) tall but not so broad as the other Wynn's, **he was of a swarthy** complexion....**his hair was coarse** (nappy) not fine.

COLONEL HUGH WYNE BY SILAS WEIR MITCHELL PG-8

WILLIAM JOHN PENN

"The lad looks like his people, when you are a man my lad you will go back to Wales to see where your people come from".

These nappy headed (coarse) Welshmen were all over the 13 colonies.... Thomas Jefferson was one of them!

"The black Basque occupied Britain from ancient times."

These black Britain's/Scotch were Roman citizens from ancient times. The word Britain and Wales is one and the same; if you have seen a Brit, you have seen a Welsh. Can a dead man speak? If he left his memoirs he can…let's hear from Thomas Jefferson.

THOMAS JEFFERSON, THOMAS JEFFERSON STUDIES, JEFFERSONS ANCESTRY

"my family came from Wales near a mountain in Snowden. My grandfather came from Chesterfield **(Wales/Britain)** in a place called Osborne's.

(1) JOURNAL OF THE ROYAL INSTITUTE OF CORNWALL

ISSUES 49-52

(2) FOOTPRINTS OF VANISHED RACES IN CORNWALL, PG-293

"**The Ivernians** were short being on average less than 5 feet inches in height. **They had** black hair, straight noses, black eyes and **dark brown skin**. The present Basque represents, according to Boyd Dawkins, **the old Ivernian race of South Wales** and are singularly like the Basque skulls. "

PRESIDENT JOHN HANCOCK

ENGRAVING LITTLEFORD AND LONDON MAGAZINE, MESSOINT
PUBLISHED IN 1775 BY C. SHEPHARD

The President of the Continental Congress and one of the signees in 1782 was none other than the illustrious **John Hancock, the black Scotch/Irish**. The closer you get to the American Revolution you begin to see that the images are black. The further away you get from the event...the pictures become white, what does this teach me? This teaches me that it was not the people from the colonial era that painted over the black images. The timeline suggests that the people guilty of this crime came from a generation closer to ours. See the black Scots on the next page.

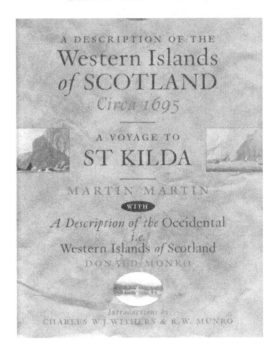

A DESCRIPTION OF THE
Western Islands
of SCOTLAND
Circa 1695

A VOYAGE TO
ST KILDA

MARTIN MARTIN
WITH
A Description of the Occidental
i.e.
Western Islands *of* Scotland
DONALD MONRO

Introductions by
CHARLES W. J. WITHERS & R. W. MUNRO

This book, <u>**a Voyage to St. Kilda**</u>, was published in the year 1695 and is only 80 years from the start of the American Revolution. These black Scots had been pouring into the 13 black British colonies since the days of King James the 6th of Scotland. Take a look at the physical description of these black Scots below.

The complexion of the islanders of Sky is most part **black.**

The complexion of the islanders of Arran is generally **brown complexion.**

The complexion of the islanders of the isle of Jura is a **black complexion.**

The complexion of the islanders of the isle of Colonsay is a **black complexion.**

The complexion of the islanders of the isle of Gigha is a **black complexion.**

I want to drive this point home, **the original people of Scotland and Wales/Welsh were black people from ancient times.** It is necessary to over emphasize this point because of the **fake history** that is being shoved down our throats. In the United States **a new phrase** has entered the consciousness of mainstream society...**fake news!** President Trump was the first President to alert the American public to this fraud. **ABC news** reporter **Michael Ross** was **suspended for the fake news** he reported **concerning** former **National Security Advisor Michael Flynn.** What is the difference between fake current history and fake colonial history? It's the same concept, one is a fake current event and the other is a fake past event. This second extreme is what we will focus on in the next chapter....the whitening of the 13 colonies.

.

CHAPTER 10: WHITENING OF THE 13 COLONIES

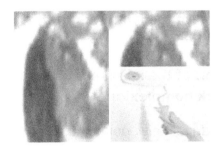

I got up at 5 A.M and went to my office **(Starbucks)** to finish editing the Negro Question Part 7. I started my workday looking at the statistics of the different ethnic groups that migrated to the 13 Colonies during the colonial era. I finished my work that morning, got in my car and drove off. That's when it hit me; Benjamin Franklin was looking at the black Europeans from France, Italy, Spain, Sweden, Germany, Scotland and Russia daily. Dr. Alexander Hamilton (Franklin's friend) confirmed my thoughts concerning Franklin's essay, when he wrote down his observations while traveling through Pennsylvania in 1744.

WHAT POLITENESS DEMANDED, ETHNIC OMISSIONS IN
FRANKLINS AUTOBIOGRAPHY PG-290

MARC L HARRIS PENN STATE UNIVERSITY

DOCTOR ALEXANDER HAMILTON PENNSYLVANIA-1744

"I dined at a tavern with a very mixed company of different nations. There were Scots, Germans, Irish, Dutch, Roman Catholics and Jews."

Franklin and Hamilton mention the same Nations but Franklin informs the reader that these Nations were swarthy/black. Are you sitting down? The next statement is going to astonish you.

WHAT POLITENESS DEMANDED, ETHNIC OMISSIONS IN FRANKLINS AUTOBIOGRAPHY PG-294

MARC L HARRIS PENN STATE UNIVERSITY

"Two other ethnic references defy classification. In one case **Franklin's narrator trades quips with political opponents** about <u>whether the Assembly's members resembled black slaves enough</u> to be sold for refusing to obey the Governor."

As you can see**.... the blackness** of the **Assembly (colonists) members** was never questioned....**they just wondered** (sarcastically) <u>**whether the assembly members were black enough**</u> to be sold as slaves. I want you to put your thinking cap on for a moment. How can blacks be assembly members, defy a Governor and write laws during colonial times, unless he was free and in charge! **These black Europeans** that Benjamin **Franklin saw everyday in the colonies** were the **seed of the black Scots and black Britain's that founded the 13 colonies.** The free black European's history has been destroyed in a very cunning manner. The establishment has merged the history of the free blacks from the North with the history of the black slave in the South. This is why it is illegal for your child not to attend school....<u>**the black child must show up to a Government funded school to learn**</u>

the merged history of the free black Europeans and the black slave from the South. He must be taught the greatest false memory of them all. He must be taught that he descended from slaves; he must never hear the history of the free black man. On this one great false memory hangs the ideology of white supremacy. The blacks in this World sit in great darkness, we are like the plants on the ground of the mighty Amazon forest, we search mightily for light but we can't find it…it is hidden from us!

SWARTHY BLACK GERMANS FLOOD PHILADELPHIA

Let's dissect this statement written in Benjamin Franklins essay; **"the Swarthy/black Germans are swarming and herding into Philadelphia".** I took the liberty of going back and looking at the population data for Philadelphia in the year 1760 and I almost fell out of my seat! See the article below.

WHAT POLITENESS DEMANDED

ETHNIC OMMISSIONS IN FRANKLIN'S AUTOBIOGRAPHY MARC L HARRIS PENN STATE UNIVERSITY PG-289

In 1723 Benjamin Franklin arrived in the city of Philadelphia. The city's population of about 5,000 people already included large numbers of Germans, Scotch-Irish, English and **Welsh inhabitants. Over the following thirty years, (1753)** Franklin became a prominent printer and then a professional public figure. The city was inundated **(overran)** by immigrants; 40,000 swarthy/black German speakers landed at Philadelphia in the period and a further

196

30,000 swarthy/black Scotch/Irish migrants entered Pennsylvania. See the data below.

WHAT POLITENESS DEMANDED ETHNIC OMMISIONS

IN BENJAMIN FRANKLINS

AUTOBIOGRAPHY

MARK HARRIS PENN STATE UNIVERSITY

"When Benjamin Franklin entered Philadelphia in 1723, there were 5000 inhabitants in the city; Welsh, Germans, English, Scots and Irish." Within 30 years 40,000 Germans and 30,000 Scot/Irish migrated to the province.

IN THE YEAR 1723	5,000	RESIDENTS IN PENNSYLVANIA
5000 SCOTS, WELSH, IRISH GERMANS		AND ENGLISH
IN THE YEAR 1753	**40,000**	**GERMAN IMMIGRANTS**
	30,000	**SCOTCH IRISH**
BLACK IMMIGRANTS	**70,000**	

THE 70,000 DOES NOT INCLUDE THE 5000 RESIDENTS FROM 1723

Franklin saw 70,000 black Germans and Scotch/Irish swarming into Pennsylvania and he described them as swarthy/black men! Since the blacks were the majority, they controlled the assembly wrote the laws and controlled the political landscape. **The state of Pennsylvania will see another black explosion** in the year 1760, see the next page.

"In the year 1700 Pennsylvania had a population of 20,000 people and one third **(6,666 black Welsh)** of Pennsylvania's population was British/Welsh.

WHAT POLITENESS DEMANDED ETHNIC OMMISIONS CONT'D

"THERE WERE 175,000 INHABITANTS IN PENNSYLVANIA IN 1760"

IN THE YEAR 1760	175,000	SEE EXPLANATION BELOW
BREAKDOWN WELSH	52,500	30% ENGLISH /WELSH IMMIGRANTS
BREAKDOWN ENGLISH	12,504	WHITE ENGLISH IMMIGRANTS
	39,996	**BLACK WELSH (BRITAIN'S) IMMIGRANTS**
	70,000	40% BLACK GERMANS/FRENCH
	52,500	30% BLACK SCOT/IRISH
		TOTAL BLACK WELSH, GERMAN, SCOT - TISH AND IRISH POPULTATION NUMBERS IN RED PRINT.
	162,496	39,996+70,000+52,500=175,000
IN THE YEAR 1700	6,666	WELSH 1/3RD OF PA, POPULATION
	6,666	
IN THE YEAR 1725	13,332	DOUBLING RATE OF 25 YEARS
	13,332	
IN THE YEAR 1750	26,664	DOUBLING RATE OF 25 YEARS
IN THE YEAR 1760	13,332	HALF THE DOUBLING RATE/ 10 YEARS
	39,996	**TOTAL WELSH BASED ON DOUBLING RATE**

Pennsylvania had a population of 175,000 residents in 1760 and **162,496 of them were black**; **39,996 were black welsh, 70,000 were black Germans, 52,500 were black Scotch Irish and** 12,504 were white **English.** The Welsh/Wales represented 1/3rd

198

(6666 black Welsh) of the population in Pennsylvania in 1700. With this information I was able to calculate the total Welsh population for Pennsylvania in 1760. **I did this by using Benjamin Franklin's doubling formula.** Once I calculated the numbers for the Welsh I was able to subtract out the numbers for the English. This is the reason Benjamin Franklin made the comment," **the number of purely white people in the World is proportionally small....the Saxons with the English make up the principal body of white people on the face of the Earth."**

The white Europeans were the minorities in the 13 British colonies based on Benjamin Franklin's doubling formula. I took the liberty of going back to 1990 to study the doubling tendencies of the white Europeans and to my dismay....they didn't double once from 1990 to the year 2000. If you can't double under pristine conditions; access to medicine, adequate food, housing, peace from wars and an educated society. How could you possibly double during colonial times...you can't.......it is impossible! **This is the reason the faces of the Generals, Colonels, Soldiers and common people have been painted white.** The Europeans are trying to make the colonial History that their fathers wrote, match the images from that era. In order to make their books balance they began painting the images white (**cooking the books**).This is what Jesus (YSHW) meant (Luke 11:52) when he said," **Woe unto you lawyers! For you have taken away the key of knowledge and them that were entering in you**

hindered." How did the establishment take away the key of knowledge? **They herded us into their schools and taught us false memories; they substituted light for darkness and darkness for light.** How have we been hindered? **The Government controls what the Government funded schools can and cannot teach....or they won't receive funding.** Once the educated whites in our generation stumbled onto the truth they understood that they had a huge problem, "our history books are full of errors, they don't match the artifacts or the memoirs...what are we to do? So instead of teaching the truth they chose the low road...**the paint brush!** This was their version of balancing the books, just like a crooked accountant would do when trying to conceal stolen client assets. Before we take a look at the numbers for the black French I would like to take a moment of your time and draw your attention to the doubling of the so called Negro. I used the same doubling formula for the so called Negro and to my dismay....we are missing 21 million Negros! In 1963 there were 20 million Negros in the United States. Per Franklin's doubling rate, the Negro population in 1988 (25 years later) should have been 40 million and 80 million strong by 2013....but that is not the case. The last census put the Negro population at 40 million which means we are short 40 million African Americans. **Let's see if we can account for the missing black people.** Since 1973 nineteen million black babies have been aborted in the United States ....that leaves 21 million missing Negros. Where could

21 million Negros be hiding? They aren't hiding and they haven't been kidnapped.....they were never born!

1963	20 MILLION NEGROS	CENSUS
1988	20 MILLION NEGROS	
	40 MILLION NEGROS	CENSUS NEGRO DOUBLED
2013	40 MILLION NEGROS	DOUBLING EVERY 25 YEARS
	80 MILLION NEGROS	IF THE NEGRO DOUBLED EVERY 25 YRS.
	.-40 MILLION NEGROS	CENSUS THE NEGRO DIDN'T DOUBLE
	.-40 MILLION NEGROS	CENSUS 40 MILLION NEGROS MISSING
	20 MILLION ▮▮▮▮	FEDERAL ABORTION STATISTICS
		20 MILLION NEGROS ABORTED
	20 MILLION	CENSUS 20 MILLION STILL MISSING
	.-20 MILLION ▮▮▮▮	THEY WERE NEVER BORN!
	0	

When couples have abortions they abort the child in their generation and the generations that should have lived.... are never born. I (Lee Cummings) am just as guilty as the other 21 million parents because I did the same thing when I was younger. The streets taught you that if you got a girl pregnant, all you had to do was get an abortion and that was that. Woman if you get pregnant as a result of fornication or adultery don't slay the child and men if you impregnate a woman don't force her to slay the child. It is not the child's fault and **there is no cloak for sin!** When you know better you should do better....right? When you are driving through your communities open your eyes and see.....there is a Planned Parenthood close to all the inner city high schools. In fact Planned

Parenthood is strategically placed all over the hood (neighborhood)....this is their little secret **(there are many secrets)**. Let's investigate the black French migrants as they swarm into the 13 colonies.

An accurate number for the migrant French flooding into the British colonies has been lost to history. Since the Germans and the French were black, the French migration totals were added to the incoming German totals.

BLACK FRENCH IMMIGRANTS ENTERING THE 13 COLONIES

FRENCH RACIAL STRAIN IN COLONIEL PENA, PG-337

Many emigrants of Huguenot (French) extraction came to Pennsylvania along with the Germans from Germany, Switzerland, from the **Palatinate**, and from **the Rhine** country generally. These had been driven from France at different times by religious persecution and a large percentage of them had become Germanized in language and customs. **Many of them had even exchanged their French names for German equivalents.** As a result of these circumstances there was a considerable number of **French immigrants to Pennsylvania who were counted among the German element of the population, whereas they were really French**. A large number of Huguenot companies came to the province on the emigrants ships from Rotterdam, whence they had **embarked after having come from Switzerland, from Alsace and Lorraine, and from**

Holland; and many such lists are on record. Inasmuch, however, **as they came on the same ships with larger numbers of Germans** and so many of them had undergone the process of Germanizing for a generation or two, <u>**they (French) were customarily lumped together with the Palatines (Germans) and their French origin was overlooked.**</u>

AM I FRENCH OR GERMAN?

AM I GERMAN OR FRENCH?

I have placed two images of two black men on this page; one is a German and the other is a Frenchman....can you tell me which one is the German and which one is the Frenchman? **The answer to this riddle can be found on pages 71 and 76.** Let us leave this matter for a moment and see the people of France thru the eyes of Benjamin Franklin.

"On the road yesterday (France) traveling to Nantes, we met six or seven country women, in company on horseback and astride. Most of the men have good complexions, **not Swarthy, like those of North France and Abbevile.**"

Benjamin Franklin was the American ambassador to France and he lived in that country for 9 long years. The man traveled around the country taking in the sights and observing the population. Franklin wrote in his diary the things he witnessed while living abroad in France..... and **Franklin's testimony is this,"** I **saw Swarthy Frenchmen when I traveled to the North of France.**"

The masses have been programmed to disregard the eyewitness account of the men and women who were alive during the colonial era. We have been taught to believe conjecture, we are taught to trust books written by men who curse the eyewitness account...shame on us.

FRENCH RACIAL STRAIN IN COLONIEL PENA, PG 337

CONT:

It is customary to regard Rupp's lists of "Thirty Thousand Immigrants" as recording the arrivals of Germans in the province, whereas a goodly percentage of these names were those of the French who accompanied the Germans to the New World.

Most of the French immigrants to Pennsylvania settled in the German counties and were absorbed by the Germans in much the same way as the early Welsh settlers were absorbed by the English. **This has led to the minimizing of the French racial strain in colonial Pennsylvania upon the part of historians.**

What does this prove? It proves that the black Germans and the French looked the same and it proves something else of greater importance. **It proves that what they label as being fact, in the Government sponsored school system, cannot be taken at face value and why**? History is an ongoing science; **ongoing means continuing or still in progress.** There are new discoveries being made daily that alter what was once considered fact. This rule was applied to the work of the great scientist Albert Einstein. When Einstein came up with his theory of relativity **(a constant universe)** it was considered a fact. Once Einstein published his findings, scientists soon discovered that the Universe was expanding at blistering speeds…Einstein's theory was no longer fact because of the ongoing rule. The black Nation's of the World have a moral obligation to apply the ongoing rule to their own history. We cannot give false memories/history as an inheritance to our children, without being partners to a lie.

COLONEL HUGH WYNE, BY SILAS WEIR MITCHELL, PG-8

WILLIAM JOHN PENN

"The lad looks like his people, when you are a man you will go back to Wales to see where your people come from".

Do you remember what Professor Boyd Dawkins said," the white barbarians pushed the Britain's west into Wales." Ancient Roman Britain was broken into two parts; Britain Primary/Prima and Britain secondary/ secunda. When the black Britain's got pushed west, they were pushed into **Britain Secondary which was renamed Wales.** See the maps with the explanation on the next page.

When looking at maps you need to take a second and focus on the different shapes of the land mass. The names might change but the shape of the land tends to remain the same. If you look at the map to your right you will see Britannia Secunda and if you look to your left you will see Wales. **Notice that the land mass is the same for Britannia Secunda and Wales**...the only thing that changed was the name....**Wales/Welsh replaced Britannia! <u>William Penn told the young black Wynne that his people were from Wales or Britain, the same place where Thomas Jefferson descended from.</u>**

The Ivernians were short, being on average less than 5 feet inches in height. **They had** black hair, straight noses, black eyes and **dark brown skin**. <u>The present Basque represents according to Boyd Dawkins the old Ivernian race of South Wales</u> and are singularly like the Basque skulls.

EDWARD THE BLACK PRINCE OF WALES/WELSH WITH EFFIGHY

WIKEPEDIA ENCYCLOPEDIA 1376 A.D

This is Edward the black British prince whose effigy mirrors his nickname. What else am I to believe?

The number of people residing in the Virginia colony slowly increased between the years 1700 to 1730 but **between the years 1730 and 1760 two hundred and forty thousand black Irish/Scots moved to Virginia**. Let's get another description of the Scotch/Irish.

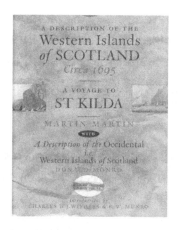

WESTERN ISLANDS OF SCOTLAND 1695

This book dated 1695 describes the black Scotch/Irish from Scotland. **The circulation date for this book, 1695**, runs concurrently **(same time)** with the colonial era. This book was written during colonial times which **make it a current event for that generation.**

The complexion of the islanders of Sky is most part **black.**

The complexion of the islanders of Arran is generally **brown complexion.**

The complexion of the islanders of the isle of Jura is a **black complexion.**

The complexion of the islanders of the isle of Colonsay is a **black complexion.**

The complexion of the islanders of the isle of Gigha is a **black complexion.**

These are the people of Scotland and as you can see, the eyewitness describes them as a black people. The Scots that were pushed into Ireland were called the Scot/Irish that is the reason they used to say if you have seen a Scot you have seen an Irishman.

SOURCE PETER H. WOODS, THE CHANGING POPULATION IN POWHATANS MANTLE: INDIANS IN THE COLONIAL SOUTHEAST (UNIVERSITY OF NEBRASKA PRESS NE 1989).

"The total population of Virginia East of the Appalachians in 1760 was 327,000 people."

This means that two thirds **(240,000 SCOTS)** of the Virginia's population in 1760 consisted of the black Scots/Irish. Have you ever sat in the midst of a brainwashed historian? They love to say that **250,000 free Negros** fought on the side of the North in the American civil war. They love to say these Negros were former slaves or that these were Negros whose masters freed them with their last dying breath. Now that we have examined the real data from the past we know that that **the narrative is foolishness**. These were the sons of the black Scots that founded the 13 colonies.

CONGRESSIONAL SERIAL, SET PG-12

"The Scot/Irish at one time formed almost the entire population of West Virginia."

This is creepy incredible…Virginia at one time was almost entirely black! **Thomas Jefferson was born in Shadwell Virginia in 1743** and **he was a descendant of the Scotch/Irish**! In 1695 the Scots were described as a black people **(PGS 209 & 210),** like I said before, 48 years is not enough time for a people's skin to change colors. All of these **black Virginians** have been **painted white, including Thomas Jefferson**, their pictures destroyed and their lands confiscated. **Your last name is the key to your poverty and your wealth!** This is the same thing that happened to the real Israelites when they went into captivity; their pictures were destroyed and their land was divided among Esau, Ishmael and Japheth. These things are understood perfectly by the brothers and sisters who walk in the light. See further proof of the black Scotch/Irish on the next page.

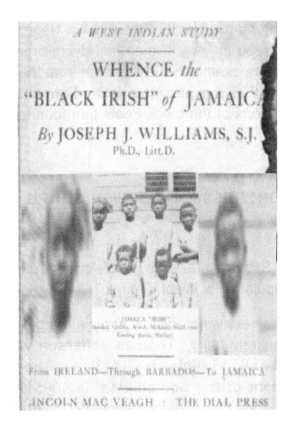

THE BLACK IRISH, AUTHOR JOSEPH J. WILLIAMS PHD.

This book was written by the Jesuit Priest Joseph Williams, in this book he states **that 100,000 black Irish children were shipped into Barbados, Jamaica and Virginia.** If you take in account that each child had a mother and a father we can now account for 300,000 black Irish/Scots. The Scotch/Irish **(Thomas Jefferson's people)** were pushed westward into Northeast Ireland by the invading whites in the year 449 A.D.

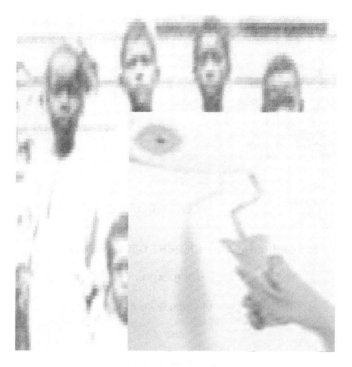

IMAGE BLOWN UP FROM PAGE 213

OLIVER CROMWELL EDICT 1653

"Those who fail to transplant themselves to **Connaught** or **Clare (Ireland)** within six months shall be guilty of high treason. **You will then be sent into America or some other part beyond the sea.**" The Royal African Company sent 249 ships to the West Indies, sending **the Irish into the Americas and West Indies.**

With **the invention of the paint brush** the distorters of the truth can **rewrite history by** simply **painting black images white.** The images of the original Scotch/Irish are now white instead of black.

THE BLACK IRISH EARLS

IMAGE OF EARL GILBERT DE CLARE 1138-1141	CLARE COAT OF ARMS

IMAGE IRISH EARL, GILBERT DECLARE 1138-1141

IMAGE LOCATION

BOOK OF TEWKESBURY ABBEY

AND

WIKEPEDIA ENCYCLOPEDIA

I decided to go into my archives and dust off the images of the black Irish Earls **(Thomas Jefferson's people)** to drive home my point. There is no disputing the blackness of these original Irish people, we simply have not been taught **real World History**. This is that ongoing science that has to be applied to colonial history or we will be just as guilty as the perpetrators of fake history.

LORD BELMONT 1ST EARL OF ANNESLY

ANNESLY COAT OF ARMS

IST EARL OF ANNESLY IRELAND, WITH ANNESLY COAT OF ARMS!

IMAGE LOCATION, CHINCESTER MONUMENTS, IRELAND

This is an image of Lord Belmont, the first Earl of Annesly, in Northern Ireland. The Annesly family coat of arms is to the left of Lord Belmont's image. The coat of arms and the image of the Earl speak for themselves.

THEOPHILUS HASTINGS

9TH EARL OF HUNTINGDON, NATIONAL PORTRAIT GALLERY COLLECTION WWWNPGORGUK

What you are witnessing first hand is <u>the correcting of Colonial history</u> and I am using the same rule that was applied to Einstein's theory of relativity....the ongoing science rule. By the year 1770 one third of Pennsylvania was populated by the black Scot/Irish. On the next page there is a spreadsheet prepared by Fogelman. It gives an **estimate** of the European immigrants swarming into the colonies. Let's dissect the numbers together.

DECADE	AFRICANS	GERMANS	NORTHERN IRISH	SOUTHERN IRISH	SCOTS	ENGLISH	WELSH	OTHER	TOTAL
1700–09	9,000	(100)	(600)	(800)	(200)	<400>	<300>	<100>	(11,500)
1710–19	10,800	(3,700)	(1,200)	(1,700)	(500)	<1,300>	<900>	<200>	(20,300)
1720–29	9,900	(2,300)	(2,100)	(3,000)	(800)	<2,200>	<1,500>	<200>	(22,000)
1730–39	40,500	13,000	4,400	7,400	(2,000)	<4,900>	<3,200>	<800>	(76,200)
1740–49	58,500	16,600	9,200	9,100	(3,100)	<7,500>	<4,900>	<1,100>	(110,000)
1750–59	49,600	29,100	14,200	8,100	(3,700)	<8,800>	<5,800>	<1,200>	(120,500)
1760–69	82,300	14,500	21,200	8,500	10,000	<11,900>	<7,800>	<1,600>	157,800
1770–75	17,800	5,200	13,200	3,900	15,000	7,100	<4,600>	<700>	67,500
Total	278,400	84,500	66,100	42,500	35,300	<44,100>	<29,000>	<5,900>	(585,800)

NOTE Figures were rounded to the nearest 100 immigrants. Estimates are divided into three categories: most accurate—no demarcation, less accurate—( ), and least accurate—< >.

Source: Fogleman 1992. "Migrations to the Thirteen British North American Colonies, 1700-1775: New Estimates." *Journal of Interdisciplinary History.*

585,800	TOTAL IMMIGRANTS	
-278400	AFRICANS	
-44000	ENGLISH	
-5900	OTHER	? DUTCH AND SWEDES
257,500	BLACK GERMANS, IRISH, SCOTS AND WELSH/WALES	

Let's use the Fogleman spreadsheet and subtract out the White English, Africans and other. We are left with a whopping total of **257,000 black Germans, Irish, Scots, Welsh/Wales, French and Dutch blacks** swarming into the colonies. Be mindful that this number does not include the original black founders of the 13 colonies who are residing in the colonies. This is what **Benjamin Franklin** was alluding to when he **said," the number of purely white people** in the World **is proportionally small."**

"The natives I shall consider in their persons, languages, manners, customs and <u>Governments.</u> **Their complexion is black** but by design **like the Gypsies in England** and using no defense against the Sun **their skin must be SWARTHY!**

Did you faint....did you fall out of your chair...are you choking on your coffee or food? You read it right....the honorable William Penn said the Europeans were black and swarthy. What does this prove? This proves that what you thought to be impossible is indeed possible; **the Europeans were still black in William Penn's generation 1644-1718.**

A JOURNAL OF A TOUR TO THE (SCOTTISH) HEBRIDES WITH SAMUEL JOHNSON

<u>AUTHOR, JAMES BOSWELL, PUBLISHED 1785 & 1810</u>
ACCURATE ACCOUNT PG-123

"There was great diversity in the faces of the circle around us: **Some were as black and wild in their appearance as any American savages whatever.** This book brings us within 2 years of the Paris Peace treaty which ended the American Revolution...this means that the Scotch/Irish, **Thomas Jefferson's people,** were still black in 1785!

The author (James Boswell-1785) states that the **Europeans that he saw from Scotland** were as **black as any American Indian** that he saw in the 13 colonies. **How do you feel about the 12 Scotts who signed the Declaration of Independence now?** William Penn said that the Indians in the 13 colonies were as black as the black Gypsies in England. Benjamin Franklin said that the Europeans were black, what else do I have to do to open your eyes? The Lord asked a question concerning his Vineyard in the book of Isaiah (Isaiah 5:1-4). Isaiah 5:1, Verse 1 Now will I sing to my well beloved a song of my beloved touching his vineyard. My well beloved has a vineyard in a very fruitful hill. Verse 2 and **he fenced it and gathered out the stones thereof** and planted it with the choicest vine and built a tower in the midst of it and also made a winepress therein. He looked that it should bring forth grapes and it brought forth wild grapes. Verse 1 And now o inhabitants of Jerusalem and men of Judah, judge, I pray you between me and my vineyard. Verse **4 what could have been done more to my vineyard that I have not done in it?** This is how I feel concerning the research in this book....what more could I have done to open your eyes? Let's see the black colonists while they are traveling to the Continental Congress. There is one problem though....their faces have been painted white.

BLACK COLONISTS TRAVELING TO THE 2ND CONTINENTAL CONGRESS

JOURNAL OF THE AMERICAN REVOLUTION

WATER COLOR PAINTING BY THOMAS SANDBY 1760

This is an image of black Colonists riding a carriage to the gathering of the Continental Congress. All of the images have been painted over with white paint...this is what they are doing...sic!

PAUL REVERE'S BLACK VERSION OF THE BOSTON MASSACRE- PAINTED 3 WEEKS AFTER THE INCIDENT!

GOVERNMENT SPONSORED VERSION OF THE BOSTON MASSACRE EVERYONE IS PAINTED WHITE!

Paul Revere's painting of the Boston massacre was painted 3 weeks after the incident and you can see that Paul Revere painted the British/German soldiers and some of the citizens black.

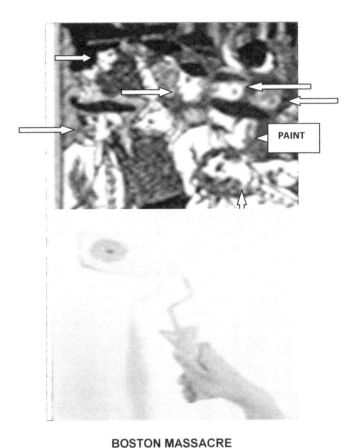

BOSTON MASSACRE

COPY OF ENGRAVING BY PAUL REVERE 1770

ARROWS POINTING TO PAINTED BLACKS

These are the same images from Paul Revere's Boston Massacre but now all of the people are white. Art is a tool that is being used to create and maintain false memories...A.K.A...moving pictures or Hollywood.

THE BOSTONIANS IN DISTRESS, LIBRARY OF CONGRESS

ENGRAVING, PHILLIP DAWE, 1774 LONDON

Check out the imagery in this picture...Bostonians in distress....the people look white right? **Wrong**....the people aren't white....their faces have been painted white to make it appear that they are white. In the book of Isaiah (Isaiah44:22) the Lord told Israel," **I have blotted out, as a thick cloud**, thy transgressions and as a cloud thy sins." The Europeans are painting black people out of World history and replacing them with false memories.

223

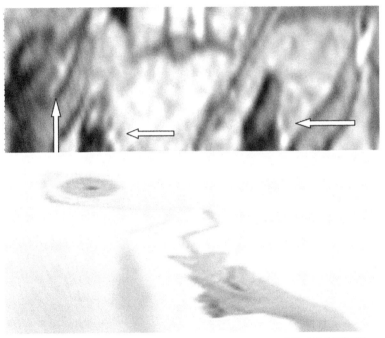

BOSTONIANS WITH PAINT ON FACES, IMAGE CROPPED FROM PG-223

I didn't major in art nor did I attend a school of art but thru a mutual friend of ours in Atlanta (Michael Israel) I was taught how to analyze images. When you are first alerted to this whitening of black art…you are a little skeptical **(I was)** but after you see artifact, after artifact that has been painted over….it finally registers. There was a time when racist Hollywood would not hire black actors so what did they do? They painted the white actors faces black; **this is how you hide the truth of a black American Revolution…white paint!**

This image could be called the class photo of the Continental Generals. I have enlarged the photo on the next page; all of the Continental, French, German, Scottish and British officer's faces have been painted white.

GEORGE WASHINGTON

THE APPEARANCE OF ALL THESE WHITE GENERALS ARE IN DIRECT OPPOSTION TO THE MEMOIRS LEFT BEHIND.

12. Count de Barras, Admiral

13. Count de Grasse, Admiral.

23. Maj. Gen. James Clinton

24. General Gist, Maryland.

14. Count Rochambeau, General in chief of the French

15. General Lincoln

16. Colonel Ebenezer Stevens, American Artillery

17. General Washington, Commander in Chief.

18. Thomas Nelson, Governor of Virginia.

19. Marquis de Lafayette.

20. Baron von Steuben.

21. Colonel Cobb, Aide-de-Camp to General Washington.

22. Colonel Trumbull

25. General Anthony Wayne

26. General Hand, Adjutant General, Pennsylvania

27. Gen. Peter Muhlenberg

28. Major General Henry Knox

29. Lt. Col. E. Huntington, Aide-de-Camp of General Lincoln.

30. Col. Timothy Pickering

31. Colonel Alexander Hamilton

32. Colonel John Laurens

33. Col. Walter Stuart, Philadelphia

34. Col. Nicholas Fish, New York

Wait a minute….hold the horses…they almost got me…..am I supposed to believe that the Colonial Officers were white because somebody painted them white? No…..the memoirs in this book present a different picture of the American Revolution. **The Memoirs on page 107** state that **General Muhlenberg** was swarthy/black. The **Memoirs on pages 183-185** state that **Colonel John Laurens** father **(Henry Laurens)** was black. The **Memoirs on page 117-124** state that **General George Washington** was Swarthy with blue eyes. **The Memoirs on page 106** state that **General Anthony Wayne** was swarthy/black. The memoirs of the men who knew these Continental generals are in direct opposition to these white portrayals.

ALL OF THESE CONTINENTAL OFFICERS HAVE THEIR FACES PAINTED WHITE!

LEE'S MEMOIR LIST OF CONTINENTAL OFFICERS

25 GENERAL ANTHONY WAYNE IRISH BLACK MAN PG-108
17 GEORGE WASHINGTON FRENCH HUGUENOT SWARTHY PGS 119-123
#32 COLONEL JOHN LAUREN FRENCH BLACK FATHER PG-190
#27 GENERAL MUHLENBERG GERMAN BLACK MAN PG-109

Do you remember our conversation about history being an ongoing science? This is what I was talking about....**the writing of Colonial history is still in progress,** On the next page I have prepared a spreadsheet that gives the Nationality of the continental officers; they are German, French,

Scotch/Irish, Dutch and Swede.....the Nations that Benjamin Franklin said were swarthy/black.

CONTINENTAL OFFICERS BLACK BY RESEARCH

#20 BARON VON STEUBEN BLACK PRUSSIAN GENERAL
#19 GENERAL MARQUIS LAFAYETTE BLACK FRENCHMAN
#22 COLONEL TRUMBULL BLACK SCOTCH IRISH
#28 MAJOR GENERAL HENRY KNOX BLACK SCOTCH IRISH
#30 COLONEL TIMOTHY PICKERING BLACK BRIT/WELSH
#31 COLONEL ALEXANDER HAMILTON BLACK SCOTCH/IRISH
#32 COLONEL JOHN LAUREN BLACK FRENCHMAN
#23 GENERAL CLINTON BLACK SCOT
#33 GENERAL WALTER STEWART BLACK SCOTCH/IRISH
34 COLONEL NICHOLAS FISH BLACK GERMAN

When I left my second office last night (Mc Donald's) I started thinking about this 2nd list of Continental Officers and it occurred to me that 5 of them had something in common....they were Scotch/Irish. The fact that there are so many Scotch/Irish officers is consistent with the contents of this book. Since the black Scots were the original founders of the 13 colonies they should have been the majority when it came to defending the land. There are **six things that the white Europeans are using to deceive the World** today; the **school system, Hollywood, History channel, museums, Church and the paint brush.** This concludes my argument concerning the whitening of the 13 colonies;

it is time to move on the Hebrew Israelites that were enslaved in the Southern states.

CHAPTER 11: JUDAH AND LEVI IN THE SOUTH

OLIVER CROMWELL IN IRELAND

Oliver Cromwell was Lord Protector of the commonwealth of England, Ireland and Scotland after the assassination of the Scottish/English King Charles the 1st. Upon taking military command of the commonwealth he invaded Ireland and history states that he committed genocide in Ireland against the black population. The black Irish that he didn't kill he had sold into the slave trade. In **1641 Cromwell had 300,000 black Irish** sold into the North Atlantic Slave Trade and in **1650 he had 100,000 Irish/Scottish children sold into Barbados**. There is an interesting law that Cromwell had published and it read;

 **OLIVER CROMWELL EDICT 1653**

"Those who fail to transplant themselves to **Connaught** or **Clare** within six months shall be guilty of high treason. <u>**You will then be sent into America or some other part beyond the sea.**</u>"

The Royal African Company sent <u>249 ships</u> to the West Indies, sending **60,000 African and Irish into the Americas and West Indies. Make no mistake about it these people are here in this Colony with us!** America is a huge colony spread out over 50 States and we have all been mingled together.

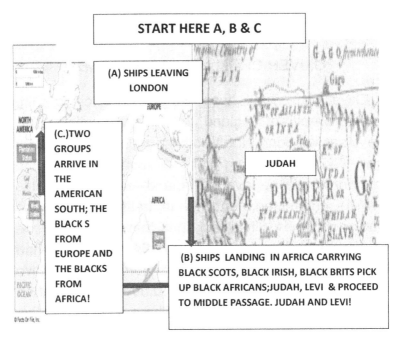

You have to remember that the 13 black British colonies are thriving and have been thriving since the days of King James the 6th of Scotland. **<u>Slavery was not recognized by the British</u>** and was illegal under the Magna Carta. **<u>This is the reason why the blacks were coming into the British colonies as indentured servants.</u>** What does the word Magna Charta mean? Magna means great and Charta means Cart.....what Cart was considered great in the history of the Jews? The Ark of the Covenant which held the 10 commandments!

This book written by the Jesuit Priest Joseph J. Williams is further proof that these people on the prisoner ships leaving London were black people! **<u>All of this information with the proof can be found written in the Negro Question Part 4 The Missing Link.</u>** Before I go any further I want to elicit the help of Professor Boyd Dawkins concerning the original inhabitants of Europe.

Professor Boyd Dawkins

Professor of Geology, Manchester University, London 1879

Our remote ancestry pages 95-106

"The original people of Britain, France, Spain and England were short black men of about 5 feet 6inches in height. They were in England when our fathers (White English) invaded the land in 449 A.D. Our fathers were a warlike people who by 607 A.D had pushed the Basque, **(black Britain's),** west into Wales, Cumberland, Westmoreland, the highlands of Scotland and Devon. **These black people boasted that they were citizens of the Roman Empire and they were!** The Welsh or ancient Britain's were in possession before the Romans ever came here. These black Basque/ Britain have brought the knowledge of **Iron and Bronze with them**. These people were herdsmen; they possessed the short horned ox, the horned sheep, the goat, pig and the horse. **Evidence of their civilization, can be seen all over the continent of Europe as well as throughout the British Islands, extending as far as the Germany and Switzerland and even to France and Spain."** These black people originated from Iberian Peninsula **and are a fragment of the old Spanish population.** They were in France, Spain, Ireland, Britain and Scotland."

232

The people of Britain and Ireland were the same people...if you have seen a black Irishman (Dub=black....dub land) you have seen a black Britain. If you want to read the research concerning this great matter you will have to purchase The Negro Question Parts 2, 4 and 6....it is the missing link to the so called Negros story! I shall add one more witness and that being the honorable Benjamin Franklin.

BENJAMIN FRANKLIN

AMERICA AS A LAND OF OPPORTUNITY

"Which leads me to add one Remark: That the Number of purely white People in the World is proportionally very small? All Africa is black or tawny. Asia chiefly tawny. America (exclusive of the new Comers) wholly so. And **in Europe, the Spaniards, Italians, French, Russians and Swedes, are generally of what we call a swarthy Complexion; as are the Germans also,** the Saxons only excepted, who with the English, make the principal Body of White People on the Face of the Earth. I could wish their Numbers were increased. And while we are, as I may call it, Scouring our Planet, by clearing America of Woods, and so making this Side of our Globe reflect a brighter Light to the Eyes of Inhabitants in mars or Venus, why should we in the Sight of Superior Beings, darken its People? Why increase the Sons of Africa, by planting them in America, where we have so fair an Opportunity, by excluding all Blacks and Tawny's, **of increasing the lovely White and**

Red? But perhaps I am partial to the complexion of my Country, for such Kind of Partiality is natural to Mankind."

With that being said we know that **there were three** different **groups of blacks** on **the slave ships** that came **into the North America**; the **black Jews of West Africa**, the **black European's** and **the black African/Hammite.** All of the blacks on these ships had one thing in common....they were all black and hence they looked alike. Since they all looked alike the great lie was forged....that they were all Africans.....this is how you make a people disappear by merging them with other people who look like them. Do you remember our conversation concerning the French and the Germans.....how the French was mistaken for the German...this is the same exact situation. This is the truth that has been hidden from the World concerning the blacks that were held captive in the South......they were the Jews of the Bible! After the American Revolution the cries of the brothers in the South reached the ears of the black Jacobites (Jacob Israel) in the North and this is a period known to the historians as the time of the Abolitionists! The French had a trading post in West Africa where they purchased or stole their captives from. Once these captives boarded the slave ships they were placed in the French colonies in North America. The Spanish did the same thing; they took their captives from their holdings in West Africa and placed them in their holdings in North America. See the spread sheet on the next few pages.

SPAINS WEST AFRICAN COLONIES

A LIST OF SPANISH COLONIES IN WEST AFRICA

BLACK WEST AFRICAN JEWS

TAKEN FROM

WHYDAH/**JUDAH**

CAPE VERDE ISLAND

GOLD COAST/**ASHANTI/LEVITES**

ANGOLA/CONGO

GAMBIA

NEW GUINEA

NIGERIA

SPAINS AFRICAN CAPTIVES

SPAINS AFRICAN JEWS DEPORTED TO SPAIN'S NORTH AMERICAN COLONIES

TAKEN TO

CALIFORNIA

SANTA FE

SAN DIEGO

SAN FRANCISCO

ST AUGUSTINE FL/**SIMEON**

NEW MEXICO

I prepared this spreadsheet for you to show you that the Spanish took their captives from their colonies in West Africa and placed their captives in their North American colonies. The place that the Europeans called the Slave Coast was originally named the Kingdom of Judah and next to it was the Ashanti or the Levite. These two tribes of Israel came into the Spanish captivity with the sons of Ham. The **Sem**inole Indian is the tribe of **Sim**eon! Sem and Sim=Shem...the E and the I are interchangeable.

235

FRANCE WEST AFRICAN COLONIES
CAPTIVES TAKEN FROM

QUIDAH/**JUDAH**
GOLD COAST/**ASHANTI**
SENEGAL
CORT DE VOIR
GUIENA
SIERRA LEONE
ASHANTI IS THE LEVITE

FRANCE WEST AFRICAN CAPTIVES
AFRICAN JEWS AND LEVITES TAKEN TO:

SOUTH CAROLINA
DETROIT
FLORIDA
TEXAS
ARKANSAS
MOBILE ALABAMA
ST LOUIS MISSOURI
ILLINOIS
LOUISIANA

1 CHRONICLES 6:1-3, 54, 57 & 59 THE LEVITES GIVEN ASHAN THESE ARE THE ASHANTI=LEVITES

JUDAH

As you can see Judah and Levi was spread out all over the Southern States by the French. In the book of Genesis (Genesis 49:10) it is written, **the scepter shall not depart from Judah or a lawgiver from between his feet,** what does this mean? It means

236

that although the 12 tribes have been scattered....Judah and Levi must remain together. Make no mistake about it.....the black Jew and the black Levite were sitting next to each other in West Africa according to the map drawn up by Emanuel Bowen in 1747. Bowen was the Royal Map Maker to King George the 2nd of England and King Louis the 15th of France. How authentic is this map? It is authentic enough to be a part of Northwestern University (Evanston Illinois) map inventory. The whites in America have known since 1747 that the black captive in the South was none other than the Jew of the Bible! Consider this picture of Sir Henry Morton Stanley crossing the Nile with an Ashanti priest. I took this image from my book the Negro Question, Who Am I. See the next page.

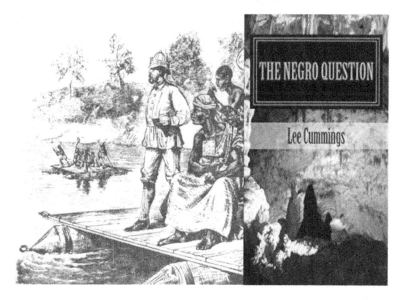

DRAWING BY SIR MORTON STANLEY

LONDON TIMES, 1894 WITH ASHANTI PRIEST/LEVITE

The most important item on this Ashanti (Levite) priest is the 12 stones around his neck. The twelve stones are a replica of the 12 stones (Exodus 28:15-21) that Aaron wore inside the tent of the tabernacle. These 12 stones represented the 12 tribes of Israel (YSRL). The whites in America and in the West know that the so called Negro is Israel. The black Europeans that fought to restore the black Stewart Kings to the throne of Britain, Scotland and Ireland were called the Jacobites. The word Jacobite is another name for Israel (see Isaiah 44:5). The English labeled this attempted coup the 15 and the 45, referencing the years of the rebellion, 1715 and 1745.

There is a publication written by Louisiana state University

Titled: Creole New Orleans

Race and Americanization

Edited by R. Hirsch and Joseph Logsdon

Louisiana State University Press

Baton Rouge and London

On page 67 of this publication are the notes of a white slaver recalling the inventory of human beings on a cargo ship.....lets' see what he writes. He writes that " sixteen slave trading ships arrived from the Senegal region. **Six ships came from Juda** and landed at the mouth of the Mississipi and <u>in 1731 one ship form</u> **JUDA** <u>landed 464 slaves at the mouth of the Mississipi.</u> **On page 69** <u>it states that</u> "**the company of India had a trading post at Juda** (Gulf of Benin) there it competed with all the nations of Europe!</u> The **Portuguese was taking the upper hand at Juda**!

Do you remember that conversation that we had earlier....the one about history being an ongoing science? This is what I am talking about...as new information comes to light it changes those things that were once considered fact. See the publication from Boston University on the next page.

A CULTURAL HISTORY OF ATLANTIC WORLD

JOHN K. THORNTON

BOSTON UNIVERSITY

CAMBRIDGE UNIVERSITY PRESS, PAGES 64 & 70

On pages 64 and 70 reference is made that **the French had a director at Whydah (Judah)** and that the French also had a trading post at Savi, the capital of (Whydah) Judah!

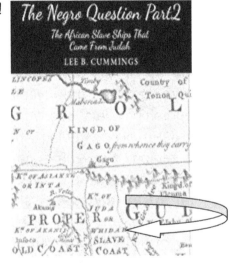

The French took captives from Whidah/Judah and dropped them off in Florida, their North American colony. Two Hebrew tribes, Judah and Levi, were taken captive to Florida by the French. We also know that the Seminole Indian, who wore fringes, is none other than Simeon of the Bible.

IACOBVS VI. SCOTLÆ REX, ET PRIMVS EO NOMINE ANGLIÆ
FRANCIÆ, ET HIBERNIÆ MAXIMO APPLAVSV ELECTVS REX &c.

This is a true image of King James the 6th of Scotland and the 1st of England; I am not interested in his blackness but I am interested in the title Iacobvs. If you use the Bible translation the word Iacobvs means Jacob or Israel. It is written in the prophets (Isaiah 44:5) one shall say, I am the Lord's **and another shall call himself by the name of Jacob** and another shall subscribe with his hand unto the Lord and surname himself by the name of Israel. There is a narrative in the book of Genesis (Genesis Chapter 32) where Jacob is wrestling with an angel and in verse 28 the angel tells Jacob," **thy name shall be called no more Jacob but Israel** for <u>**as a prince has thou power with God and with men**</u> and hast prevailed. King James of Scotland and England also designed the English flag...some say the cross is a Roman death symbol but I see the Hebrew Taw.

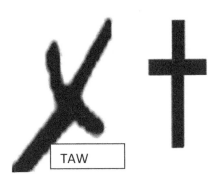

TAW

HEBREW TAW MEANS TWO

The Hebrew Taw lays sideways, the Gentiles simply stood the Taw up vertically and called it a t....they actually called it a t which is short for two or taw...think about it. One day the Most High made this plain to me while reading the book of Ezekiel;" thou **son of man <u>take thee one stick and write upon it for Judah </u>and for the children of Israel his companions: <u>Then take another stick and write upon it for Joseph, the stick of Ephraim</u> and for all the house of Israel his companions** Vs 17 and join **<u>them one to another into one stick</u> and they shall become one in thine hand.** Vs 19 Say unto them,

242

thus saith the Lord God behold I will take the stick of Joseph which is in the hand of Ephraim and the tribes of Israel his fellows and will put them with him even with the stick of Judah and make them one stick and they shall be one in mine hand. **We were taught to read alphabets but we were never taught to read signs and artifacts!** When King James had the name Jacobus written on his image he was sending a message into future that he was an Israelite King. The combining of the two sticks (Taw or Cross) was a sign that he was the King over Judah and Israel! The Scotch/Irish were black Jacobites or Hebrew Israelites. King James was not the only Israelite Scottish King, see the list below.

KING JAMES 1ST OF SCOTLAND JACOBUS	1406-1437	
KING JAMES 2ND OF SCOTLAND JACOBUS	1437-1460	
KING JAMES 3RD OF SCOTLAND JACOBUS	1460-1488	
KING JAMES 4TH OF SCOTLAND JACOBUS	1488-1513	
KING JAMES 5TH OF SCOTLAND JACOBUS	1513-1542	

JACOBITE KINGS OF SCOTLAND

THE HIGHLANDERS

INSCRIPTION HISTORICA REGVM SCOTORVM

ICONOGRAPHIA SCOTTICA JOHN PINKERTON 1797

There were 4 Jacobite Kings and 1 German Hanover King that founded the original 13 Colonies. I have made that research available in the Negro Question part 6.

THE ORIGINAL 13 COLONIES

1-VIRGINIA (1607)
2-MASSACHUSETTS (1620)
3- NEW HAMPSHIRE (1623)
4-NEW YORK (1625) (1664)
5-MARYLAND (1632)
6-CONNECTICUT (1636)
7-RHODE ISLAND (1636)
8-DELAWARE (1638)
9-NORTH CAROLINA (1663)
10-NEW JERSEY(1664)
11-SOUTH CAROLINA (1664)
12-PENNSYLVANIA (1681)
13-GEORGIA (1732)

KING JAMES 6TH OF SCOTLAND

FOUNDED VIRGINIA

FOUNDED MASSACHUSETTS/NEW HAMPS

FOUNDED NEW ENGLAND

KING CHARLES 2ND OF ENGLAND

FOUNDED CONNECTICUT

FOUNDED RHODE ISLAND

FOUNDED DELAWARE

FOUNDED NTH CAROLINA

FOUNDED NEW JERSEY

FOUNDED SOUTH CAROLINA

FOUNDED PENNSYLVIA

FOUNDED NEW YORK

FOUNDED MASSACHUSETTS

KING GEORGE 2ND OF ENGLAND   FOUNDED GEORGIA

All of these Kings were black Scottish Highlander Kings with the exception of King George who was a black Hanover German King. This subject is explained in greater detail in the Negro Question Part 6-The 13 Black Colonies. I apologize for reintroducing material from the other books but I have no other research to borrow from....so I have to borrow from my own research.

JACOBITE UPRISINGS OF 1715 AND 1745

The Jacobite **(Hebrew Israelites)** risings, also known as the Jacobite rebellions or the War of the British Succession were a series of uprisings, rebellions, and wars in Britain and Ireland occurring between 1688 and 1746. The uprisings had the aim of returning the black Scottish Jacobite Kings **(Israelite Kings)** back to the thrones of Scotland, Ireland and Britain. This series of conflicts takes its name Jacobitism, from Jacobus which is Hebrew for Jacob. The major Jacobite risings were called the Jacobite rebellions by the ruling governments. The "first Jacobite rebellion" and "second Jacobite rebellion" were also known respectively as **"the Fifteen" and "the Forty-five"**, after the years in which they occurred (1715 and 1745). After the House of Hanover succeeded to the British throne in 1714, the risings continued and intensified. They continued until the last Jacobite rebellion ("the Forty-five"), led by Charles Edward Stuart and were soundly defeated at the Battle of Culloden in 1746. **There is a description** of these **black Jacobites** (Hebrew Israelites) as they are being deported in 1745. **See the ships manifest below.**

SHIPS MANIFEST THE VETERAN 1745

FIRST	LAST NAME	AGE	COLOR
ROBERT	ADAM	18	BROWN
WILLIAM	BELL	46	BLACK
DOUGALL	CAMPBELL	18	BROWN
ALEXANDER	CATTANACH	17	BLACK
DOUGALL	CAMPBELL	18	BROWN
ALEXANDER	CAMPBELL	18	BROWN
JOHN	CAMPBELL	20	BROWN
ALEXANDER	**CAMERON**	19	BROWN
ALEXANDER	DAVIDSON	17	RUDDY
ANDREW	EDWARDS	24	BLACK
JOHN	GORDON	19	BLACK
ALEXANDER	GOODBRAND	30	BLACK
JOHN	GRANT	40	BLACK
ALEXANDER	GRANT	25	BROWN
JOSEPH	HINCHLIFF	30	BLACK
JOHN	JOHNSON	30	BROWN
DAVID	JOINER	20	BROWN
JOHN	KENNEDY	32	BLACK
GEORGE	KEITH	32	BLACK
WILLIAM	MCCLEAN	32	RUDDY
ANGUS	MCINTOSH	26	BLACK
PETER	MCINTOSH	34	BROWN

INFORMATION CAN BE FOUND IN THE BOOK;

JACOBITE GLEANINGS FROM STATE MANUSCRIPTS, PAGE 48

AUTHOR J.MACBETH FORBES, HARVARD COLLEGE LIBRARY

These black Israelites were absorbed by the original black colonists and fought against the British in the American Revolution. **This ships manifest validates John Mackey's** description of the Scottish Nobles, **William Penn's description of the black gypsy Europeans and** Benjamin Franklin's **statement that the European's were black.**

FIRST	LAST NAME	AGE		REMARKS
ANGUS	MCINTOSH	26		BLACK
PETER	MCINTOSH	34		BROWN
JAMES	MCPHEARSON	22		BLACK
ALEXANDER	**MCLEOD**	**18**	**XXXXXXX**	BROWN
CHARLES	MORGAN	18		BROWN
DONALD	MCGILLIS	18		BLACK
ALLEN	MCDOUGALL	26		BLACK
ANGUS	MCDONALD	60		BLACK
ALEXANDER	MARNOCK	26		BROWN
GEORGE	NICHOLL	26		BROWN
JAMES	NIELSON	26	SWARTHY	BLACK
JAMES	LACKEY	16		BLACK
GEORGE	BAIN	25	SWARTHY	BLACK
HECTOR	MCGILLIS	16		BLACK
JOHN	**STEWART**	**18**	**XXXXXXX**	BROWN
JOHN	THOMPSON	18		BLACK
ISABELL	CHAMBERS	25	TALL	BLACK

INFORMATION CAN BE FOUND IN THE BOOK;

JACOBITE GLEANINGS FROM STATE MANUSCRIPTS, PAGE 48

AUTHOR J.MACBETH FORBES, HARVARD COLLEGE LIBRARY

I want to slow this discussion down for one minute to make a point. Although they destroyed the black images from the colonial era, this ships manifest gives an accurate description of what the colonists really looked like. These black Jacobite colonists became the black Continental army that fought against the black British/Germany army that invaded the 13 colonies. This is the reason you have white paint on all of the images from the Colonial era....it is a coverup! This is the real history of America and the 13 colonies....haven't you ever wondered why there were 13 stars on the U.S flag?

IN 1777 THE AMERICAN FLAG; 13 STARS

Go to your Bible and read Revelation (Revelation 12:1,2,4&5) and see where it was written," And there appeared a great wonder in heaven; a woman clothed with the sun and the moon under her feet and upon her head **a crown of twelve stars.** Then go to Genesis (Genesis 37:5, 9) Verse 5 and Joseph dreamed a dream and he told it his brethren and they hated him yet the more. Verse 9 and he dreamed yet another dream and told it his brethren and said, behold I have dreamed a dream more; and behold the sun and the moon and the eleven stars made obeisance to me. In the 12th chapter of Revelation there were twelve stars which represented the 12 tribes of Israel but Joseph said," the 11 stars made obeisance to me,"....the reason one star is missing is because it is Joseph...he is the 12th star. Joseph was given a double portion and this may be the reason that the flag had 13 stars on it. This is a sign to the brothers who have real knowledge; a novice won't know these things! I have a greater witness than this come and see.

HISTORICAL SOCIETY OF MONTGOMERY COUNTY

HISTORICAL SKETCHES A COLLECTION OF PAPERS
VOLUME 2 PAGE- 226

THE COLONISTS WORE FRINGES

"**Several Hessian prisoners (Germans)** had been brought to Philadelphia. **One of them accidently met a settler who happened to be his first cousin (40,000 Black Germans migrated to Philadelphia)** who asked him, what induced him to come to America to injure his own flesh and blood? Others being asked said that <u>the English officers (black British German officers) made them to think that the colonists were savages</u>....**<u>especially those who had fringes on their dress/garments.</u>**" Why do the colonists have fringes on their garments? Nobody wore fringes (Numbers 15:38-41) but the Hebrew Israelites of the Bible. Numbers 15:38 Speak unto the children of Israel that they make them fringes in the borders of their garments **throughout their generations.** Verse 39 and it shall be unto you for a fringe that you may look upon it and remember all the commandments of the (YHWH) Lord and do them. These are the black Jacobites that were deported into the 13 colonies during the uprising of 1715 and 1745...this is consistent with real colonial history. To this very day, **December 15, 2017**, the black Jacobites (Hebrews) wear fringes to the Sabbath classes. When we started this journey our focus was on the **great argument....the memoirs of a black American Revolution.** It took me 250 pages to present my argument and now it is your turn. What does he mean my turn? You get to judge the research presented in this book verses the narrative given to us by the Government sponsored school system. I remember when Pontius Pilate was judging Jesus (YSHW) and I thought to myself, "This man is not worthy to judge the Messiah." This is how I feel about academia, their eyes have been blinded and their minds have been dulled by the false memories they were forced to memorize. The very institutions that they trust in have disqualified them from being our teachers. You on the other hand, you are my equals, peers, brethren and soldiers of the 1st rank! I count it an honor to be judged by you because I know you...your weights and balances are just.

CONCLUSION

The first man to write as an eyewitness was the ancient Sumerians...they wrote their testimony (eyewitness) on baked clay using reeds as pens. Some of the World's greatest archaeological finds found in Mesopotamia are credited to these memoirs written on clay tablets. We credit the Hebrew Israelites with the Magna Charta, **royal law, which** was written on stone. These 10 commandments have become the legal code of every civilized Government on this planet. The memoirs painted on the walls of the Chauvet cave in Ardeche France have been received with great enthusiasm. Each generation had an eyewitness... someone who was present at the scene. The Apostles were eyewitnesses to the crucifixion of the Hebrew Messiah. The colonial era was full of men and women who could read and write...what a bonus. **The memoirs of the people who lived during the colonial period are not allowed in the Government sponsored school system.** How can this be? If the Ox that treads the corn has a right to eat....shouldn't the memoirs of the colonists and Generals be read in our schools? The original black colonists fought and died for this principal called freedom...yet their memoirs (eyewitness account) are denied access to the very schools that their deaths help create. With that being said let's end this great discussion with the memoirs of the people that were alive during the American Revolution. **Conclusion continued on next page.**

CONCLUSION CONT'D

BRITISH PRIME MINISTER CHARLES FOX

THE ATLANTIC MONTHLY VOLUMNE 105 PG 447

"Charles's Fox is a short fat and gross man with a swarthy complexion and dark.

MEMOIRS OF GENERAL KEPPEL

THE EDINBURGH REVIEW, VOLUMES 143-144, PAGE 235

" A greater man than Robert Adair lives in Lord Albermales recollections. **It must have been in the summer of 1806, when he was about 7 years old that his father took him to see Mr. Fox**. In many respects his personal appearance differed little from the many pictures and prints of him. **His face had lost its swarthy appearance which in the caricatures of that day obtained him the name Nigger**".

BRITISH ADMIRAL RICHARD BLACK DICK HOWE, PG-47

ENCYCLOPEDIA BRITANNICA A DICTIONARY OF ARTS SCIENCES VOLUMES 13 & 14 PAGE-837

"Admiral Richard Howe's nickname was given to him on account of his **SWARTHY complexion.**

COMMANDER IN CHIEF WILLIAM HOWE

AUTHOR JOHN S. PANCAKE, UNIVERSITY OF ALABAMA PRESS

"THE TALL SWARTHY HOWE BROTHERS"

(1) THE AMERICAN REVOLUTION 100, THE BATTLES, PEOPLE AND EVENTS OF THE AMERICAN REVOLUTION, PG-58

"Commander William Howe was Swarthy, 6ft tall with bad teeth."

BRITISH AIDE DE CAMP LORD RAWDON

WITH WASHINGTON AT VALLEY FORGEBY WALTER BETRAM
FOSTER PG-237

BRITISH AIDE DE CAMP LORD RAWDON

"Lord **Rawdon** that **Swarthy** haughty nobleman, both hated and feared by all that came in contact with him was quartered to Peter Reeve's house."

BRITISH GENERAL BANASTRE TARLETON

WASHINGTON AND HIS COUNTRY. BEING IRVINGS LIFE OF
WASHINGTON BEING ABRIDGED PG-381

"This bold dragon **(General Banastre Tarleton)** so noted in Southern warfare, was about 26 years of age, **was of a swarthy complexion** with small black piercing eyes. **GENERAL.**

KING LOUIS XIV FRANCE

KINGS BODY LOCATION ABBY OF SAINT DENIS

FRENCH NATIONAL MUSEUM OF MONUMENTS

"King Louis XIV skin was so black that it looked like ink."

MEMOIRS OF THOMAS JEFFERSON FRANCE

THE STORMING OF THE BASTILE

"60,000 FRENCHMEN OF ALL COLORS"

"The king of France came to Paris, leaving the queen in consternation for his return. Omitting the less important figures of the procession, I will only observe that the king's carriage was in the center, on each side of it the States general, in two ranks, afoot, at their head the Marquis de la Fayette as commander in chief, on horseback, and Bourgeois guards before and behind. I witnessed 60,000 citizens (French Citizens) of all forms and colors."

255

CONTINENTAL COLONEL HUGH WYNE

REFERENCE BOOK

COLONEL HUGH WYNE, BY SILAS WEIR MITCHELL PG-125

"We all rose as he drew near, my mother saying in my ear as he approached; "now Hugh, it is Arthur Wynn, now Hugh take care. **This newly found cousin was like all of us** (Wynn family) tall but not so broad as the other Wynn's, **he was of a swarthy complexion**....his hair was coarse (nappy) not fine."

WILLIAM PENN

"Son when you get older you will go back to Wales to see where your people come from"

MEMOIRS THOMAS HICKEY

WHETHERSFIELD HISTORICAL SOCIETY

CHAPTER 6 PAGE 30 & 32

"Thomas Hickey, has been described as 'a dark complexioned man of five feet six, well set ... an Irishman and hitherto a deserter from the British Army."

CONTINENTAL GENERAL ANTHONY WAYNE

VALLEY FORGE A CHRONICLE OF HEROISM

CHAPTER 6 PGS 31, 32

"There 'he is, at this moment, riding up the hill from his quarters in the valley. **A man of medium height and strong frame, he sits his horse well and with a dashing air. His nose is prominent, his eye piercing, his complexion ruddy,** he has in him the qualities of a great general, as he shall show many a time in his short life of one-and-fifty years, **General Anthoney Wayne.**"

GENERAL MUHLENBERG

MEMOIRS OF HENRY ARMITT BROWN TOGETHER WITH FOUR ORACLE ORATIONS PG-329

"at the corner of the entrenchments by the river, is the Virginia Brigade of Muhlenberg. Born at the Trappe close by and educated abroad, **Muhlenberg** was a **clergyman in Virginia** when the war came on, but he has doffed his parson's gownforever **for the buff and blue of a brigadier. His stalwart form and swarthy face** are already as familiar to the enemy as they are to his own men.

CONTINENTAL GENERAL MARION

MEMOIRS OF HENRY ARMITT BROWN TOGETHER WITH FOUR ORACLE ORATIONS PG-329

AND A FEW BLOODY NOSES THE REALITIES AND MYTHOLOGIES OF THE AMERCIAN REVOLUTION

IMAGE-SOUTH CAROLINA VIRTURAL LIBRARY

"When **Marion** arrived at the makeshift camp, he wore a crimson jacket and a leather cap with a silver crescent inscribed with the words "Liberty or Death." He was a stranger to the officers and men, and they flocked about him to obtain a sight of their future commander," recalled William James, who joined Marion's men when he was only 15. "**He was rather below the middle stature, lean and swarthy** (Swarthy means Black).

BRIGADIER GENERAL JOHN SULLIVAN

MEMOIRS OF

HENRY ARMITT BROWN

TOGETHER WITH 4 HISTORICAL ORATIONS, YALE UNIVERITY

"**Swarthy John Sullivan** is a little headstrong but brave as a lion."

CAPTAIN PAUL JONES

MEMOIRS OF THE MARQUEE OF ROCKINHAM AND HIS CONTEMPORARIES VOL 2 PAGE-379

"An adventurer with a single ship caused an almost consternation in the North. I mean **Paul Jones.** This celebrated renegade from Scotland **was a short thick set man with coarse features and swarthy complexion.**"

CAPTAIN PAUL JONES CONT:

APPLETON'S MAGAZINE VOL 6 PG-116

   "Captain Paul Jones hair and eyebrows are black and his eyes are large, brilliant, piercing....**his complexion is Swarthy**...almost **like that of a Moor!**

GENERAL CHARLES LEE

WASHINGTON AND HIS GENERALS OR LEGENDS OF THE AMERICAN REVOLUTION VOL 1 AUTHOR GEORGE LIPPARD PAGE-33

" The one who held the map was tall and straight shouldered and I knew the figure to be that of the General in chief, as I approached I recognized too, the **Swarthy face of General Charles Lee."**

GENERAL LIGHTHORSE HENRY LEE

FRANK LESLIES ILLUSTRATED NEWSPAPER

VOL 41-43 MAY13, 1876 PAGE 162

"The **Ruddy** Virginian Light horse Henry Lee".

POLISH GENERAL PULASKI

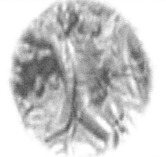

WASHINGTON AND HIS GENERALS OR LEGENDS OF THE AMERICAN REVOLUTION VOL 1, PG-39

"Ha **that gallant band whom comes trooping on**, spurring their stout steeds with wild haunches.....**every SWARTHY hand raising the sword** on high.....**they wear the look of foreigners**...trained to fight in the exterminating wars of Europe. Their leader, **Pulaski,** is tall and proportioned with a **Dark Hued face** (Hued=Color). This is the band of General Pulaski!

HUGH WYNNE THE FREE QUAKER PG-463

"General Washington has blue eyes and ruddy skin".

Washington has blue eyes and ruddy skin.

BENEDICT ARNOLD

HUGH WYNNE THE FREE QUAKER PG-385

"Major Arnold is a **DARK man** and **yet Ruddy** with a large nose".

BOSTON MAGAZINE 1784, JOHN NORMAN

THE HANGING OF THOMAS JEREMIAH A FREE BLACK MANS
ENCOUNTER WITH LIBERTY PG-21

"Nothing better exemplifies the intimate connection between the slave trade and the rise of Charles town's gentry than the career of Henry Laurens. **<u>Elkanah Watson a young American Merchant who met Henry Laurens in France in 1782</u>** remembered him as a pleasant and facetious gentleman of **SWARTHY complexion**, medium size and slender form."

PRESIDENT HENRY LAURENS OF CONGRESS

MEN AND TIMES OF THE REVOLUTION: OR MEMOIRS OF ELKANAH WATSON PG 138 & 139

"**Mr. Laurens (Henry Laurens) was formerly President of Congress** and **was appointed ambassador to Holland.** He was a citizen of South Carolina, a man of great wealth and position. **He had a swarthy complexion,** medium size and slender form." I was set off with Mr. Lauren who was in my vicinity

ROBERT SOUTHEY'S COLLECTION OF LETTERS

LETTERS #24

Then skin and hair color and names (Letter 24). **Southey offers the idea that the complexions and hair colors of English people show their favorite myths about their origins of themselves cannot be.** If Celts had fair hair and eyes, **WHERE DOES ALL THIS DARK HAIR, DARK EYES AND SWARTHY SKIN COME FROM?**

ANNOUNCEMENTS AFTER REFERENCES!

REFERENCES

CHARLES JAMES FOX ATLANTIC MONTHLY VOL 105- PG-26
PG-447.

CHARLES JAMES FOX STATUE-10 DOWNING ST, ENG PG-28

CHARLES STEWART, WESTMINSTR MUSEUM, ENG   PG-27

WILLIAM PITT, NATIONAL PORTRAIT GALLERY   PG-30

WILLIAM PITT, CARICATURE BRITISH POLITICAL -   PG-31,32
CARTOONS 1780.

JOHN WILKES, BRITISH MUSEUM   PG-35,36

LORD NORTH, BRITISH POLITICAL -   PG-37
CARTOONS, 1775.

CHIEF JUSTICE MANSFIELD, BRITISH POLITICAL -   PG-38,82
CARTOONS, 1775.

PALEO HEBREW INSCRIPTION, WIKEPEDIA   PG-39

HENRY GRENVILLE, 1763 MONTHLY MIRROR   PG-41

CHARLES PRATT, ENGRAVER JOHN FABER, LONDON-   PG-42

MAYOR CROSBY & ALDERMAN RICH OLIVER-   PG-43
LONDON MAGAZINE.

QUEEN CHARLOTTE, NATIONAL PORTRAIT GALLERY   PG-44

GENERAL LORD CORNWALLIS, THE HISTORY OF THE-   PG-45
WAR FROM THE COMMENCEMENT OF THE FRENCH-
REVOLUTION TO THE PRESENT TIME, VOL 1 -
AUTHOR HEWSON CLARK.

DUKE OF YORK, NATIONAL PORTRAIT GALLERY 1664   PG-47

ADMIRAL RICHARD HOWE, ENGRAVER J. COPELY   PG-48,49

HENRY CLINTON, BRITISH PRINTS, LIB OF CONGRESS   PG-50

LORD FRANCIS RAWDON, WITH WASHINGTON AT -   PG-51
VALLEY FORGE, WALTER FOSTER, PG 237.

REFERENCES CONT'D

BANASTRE TARLETON, LIBRARY OF CONGRESS 1782- PG-52,53
AND THE WESTMINSTER MAGAZINE

GENERAL KNYPHAUSEN, WIKEPEDIA   PG-54

BENEDICT ARNOLD, HUGE WYNNE THE -   PG-55
FREE QUAKER, PG-385.

QUEEN ISABELLA OF FRANCE, BRITISH LIBRARY -   PG-56
MS14EIVFOL.316V.

QUEEN ISABELLA , ALEYMA.TUMBIR.COM   PG-57

KING SANCHO OF PAMPHILLIA/NAVARRA-   PG-57
INDEX OF ROYAL ROYAL PRIVALEGES.

KING LOUIS XIV OF FRANCE, FRENCH NATIONAL-   PG-58
MUSEUM OF MONUMENTS, ABBEY OF ST. DENIS.

PRINCESS LOUISE MARIE THRESA, LIBRARY OF -   PG-59
GRENVIEW, PARIS FRANCE.

COURT OF VERSAILLES, MEMOIRS OF -   PG-60
DUC OF SIMON.

KING CHARLES 5TH OF FRANCE, HISTORIE DE-   PG-64
DU GUESCLIN, FRANCE.

SHRINE OF CHARLEMAGNE, AACHEN CATHEDRAL-   PG-65-66
GERMANY.   PG-68,69

SKELETAL REMAINS, MONOPRIX MARKET-   PG-67,68
NORTHERN FRANCE, WIKEPEDIA.

GENERAL CHARLES COMTE ESTANG, NY LIBRARY   PG-72

GENERAL ALEXANDER DUMAS, WIKEPEDIA   PG-73

ALEXANDER DUMAS, WIKEPEDIA   PG-74

GERMAN DUKE, GEORGE WILLIAM, WIKEPEDIA   PG-76,77

HAITIAN ARMY, THE HAITIAN REVOLUTION-   PG-78
AUTHOR DAVID GEGGUS

REFERENCES CONT'D

COLUMN OF MARCUS AURELIUS, ROME ITALY — PG-83,84

ROMANS, DURA EUROPA SYNAGOGUE, SYRIA — PG-85

CHARLES OF BIRKENFELD ZWIEBUCKEN, HISTORY-
OF BIRKENFELD. — PG-88

PRINCE PHILLIP LANDGRAVE, COUNT HESSE — PG-89

PRINCE MAURICE LANDGRAVE, BIBLOTHECA -
CHALCOGRAPHICA. — PG-90

GERMAN HESSIAN DRUMMER BOY — PG-91

LANDGRAVE WILLIAM HESSE, MAUSOLEUM-
RUPENHEIM GERMANY. — PG-92

WORLD TURNED UPSIDE DOWN, AUTHOR-
RICHARD FERRIE. — PG-94

KING JAMES, NEW COLLEGE EDINBURG, UK — PG-97

FREDERICK 5TH OF BOHEMIA, ENGRAVER WILEM-
JAKOBEZS DELFF. — PG-98,99

QUEEN ELIZABETH STEWART, ANCIENT MISC-
SAXONY COINS. — PG-98,99

ERNST AUGUST STATUE, MARIAN CASTLE LOWER-
SAXONY GERMANY. — PG-100

ADMIRAL RICHARD HOWE, NATIONAL -
PORTRAIT GALLERY. — PG-101

COMMANDER WILLIAM HOWE, NATIONAL-
PORTRAIT GALLERY. — PG-101

COLONEL HUGHE WYNNE, HUGHE WYNNE THE-
FREE QUAKER, PG-24. — PG-104

GENERAL WAYNE, STONEY POINT MEDAL

GENERAL MUHLENBERG, STATUE SHANDANDOAH-
VIRGINIA COURTHOUSE. — PG-107

REFERENCES CONT'D

GENERAL FRANCIS MARION, SOUTH CAROLINA -   PG-108
VIRTUAL LIBRARY .

GENERAL JOHN SULLIVAN, YALE UNIVERSITY   PG-109

CAPTAIN PAUL JONES, MEMOIRS OF THE MARQUE- PG-110
OF ROCKINGHAM & HIS CONTEMPORARIES -
VOL 2, PG-379.

CAPTAIN PAUL JONES, APPLETON MAGAZINE-   PG-111
VOL 6, PG-116.

GENERAL CHARLES LEE, WASHINGTON AND HIS-   PG-112
GENERALS OR LEGENDS OF THE AMERICAN-
REVOLUTION, VOL 1, LIPPARD, PG-33.

GENERAL HENRY LEE, FRANK LESLIES ILLUSTRATED- PG-113
NEWSPAPER.

BARON VON STEUBEN, STATUE NATIONAL -   PG-114,115
HISTORIC PARK PENNSYLVANIA.

GENERAL PULASKI, STATUE PATTERSON PARK-   PG-116
BALTIMORE MARYLAND.

BENEDICT ARNOLD, LIBRARY OF CONGRESS PRINTS- PG-119
AND PHOTOGRAPH DIVISION-FROM ORIGINAL -
ITEM, REPRODUCTION ID# LC-DIG-PGA-10525.

GENERAL GEORGE WASHINGTON, LIBRARY-   PG-120
OF CONGRESS.

GEORGE WASHINGTON, STATUE, ILE DE RE FRANCE- PG-121,122
COGNACK MUSEUM FRANCE.   & PG-123

BATTLE OF LAKE GEORGE, RICHARD H. BROWN-   PG-125,126
COLLECTION & SAMUEL BLODGET LONDON 1756.   & PG-127

BLACK INDIANS, HISTORICAL CARICATURE OF -   PG-128,129
THE CHEROKEE NATION, LIBRARY OF CONGRESS.   PG-130
PRESIDENT ANDREW JACKSON, LITHOGRAPH-
LIBRARY OF CONGRESS.

REFERENCES CONT'D

BLACK AMERICAN INDIANS, BENJAMIN FRANKLIN- PG-132
COLLECTION, LIBRARY OF CONGRESS.

BRITAIN POLITICAL CARTOON 1780, CATALOGUE- PG-133
PRINTS & DRAWINGS, BRITISH MUSEUM, BM5989
REFERENCE-AMERICAN REVOLUTION IN DRAWINGS.

LANDING OF THE BRITISH TROOPS, PAUL REVERE- PG-134,135
THE AMERICAN ANTIQUARIAN SOCIETY, LIBRARY - & PG-136
OF CONGRESS.

BOSTON MASSACRE, PAUL REVERE, LIBRARY OF- PG-137,138
CONGRESS.

FRANCAIS DU FUW TERRIBLE NOUVELLE YORCK- PG-140,141
NEW YORK PUBLIC LIBRARY- & PG-144
IMAGE ID-PSNYPL-PRN-972URL.

BURNING OF CHARLESTON, WIKEPEDIA PG-148

MARQUIS LAFAYETTE, WIDEPEDIA PG-149

CONTINENTAL SOLDIERS PG-150

GENERAL CLINTON PG-152

GENERAL COMTE' DE ESTAING PG-157

GENERAL JOHN SULLIVAN, NEW HAMPSHIRE- PG-158
LIBRARY AND THE LIBRARY OF CONGRESS.

BATTLE OF WHITE MARSH, LIBRARY OF CONGRESS- PG-160
GEOGRAPHY & MAP DIVISION.

BLACK BRITISH GERMAN ARTILLARY MEN LIBRARY- PG-162
OF CONGRESS.

REFERENCES CONT'D

PROFESSOR BOYD DAWKINS, WIKEPEDIA   PG-167

FLORA MAC DONALD, STATUE, INVERNESS-CASTLE, UK & WIKEPEDIA.   PG-173

MARSHALL ETIENNE JACQUES MAC DONALD-ON THE SIDE OF LOUVRE ON RUE DE RIVOLI-PARIS, FRANCE.   PG-174

BLACK CONTINENTAL SOLDIERS, BROWN-UNIVERSITY.   PG-175

PATRIOTIC BARBER, BRITISH MUSEUM   PG-176

BLACK SAM'S TAVERN, WIKEPEDIA   PG-179

LADY AMERICA, BRITAIN CARTOON & PRINTS AND LIBRARY OF CONGRESS.   PG-179,181

PRESIDENT HENRY LAUREN, BOSTON-MAGAZINE, 1784, ENGRAVER JOHN NORMAN.   PG-182

DECLARATION OF INDEPENDENCE MEDAL-JOHN BULL AND WIKEPEDIA ENCYCLOPEDIA.   PG-186

HUGHE WYNNE, HUGHE WYNNE THE FREE-QUAKER.   PG-189

PRESIDENT JOHN HANCOCK, LONDON -MAGAZINE, MESSOINT 1775 C. SHEPPARD.   PG-191

EDWARD THE BLACK PRINCE, WIKEPEDIA   PG-208

THE BLACK IRISH, JOSEPH J. WILLIAMS   PG-212

IRISH EARL GILBERT DE CLARE, BOOK-OF TEWKESBURY AND WIKEPEDIA.   PG-214

LORD BELMONT, STATUE, CHINCESTER-MONUMENTS, IRELAND.   PG-215

EARL THEOPHILUS HASTINGS, NATIONAL PORTRAIT- PG-216
GALLERY AND COLLECTION WWW.NPGORGUK.
COLONISTS TRAVEL TO CONTINENTAL CONGRESS-   PG-220
JOURNAL OF THE AMERICAN REVOLUTION.
AMERICAN FLAG, WIKEPEDIA   PG-248

ANNOUNCEMENTS ON NEXT PAGE!

ANNOUNCEMENTS!!

NEGRO QUESTION ONLINE BOOKSTORE

URL-NEGROQUESTIONBOOKSTORE

The Negro Question Book series has created its first online bookstore where you can buy autographed books at a discount from the author. Website info= **negroquestionbookstore** or copy and paste leecummingsauthorthenegroquestion.com/ in your Google bar.

THE NEGRO QUESTION ONLINE HISTORY CLASS

COST OF COURSE $150 FOOR 6 WEEKS
THIS COMES OUT TO $25 PER WEEK

CONTACT LEE CUMMINGS FOR MORE INFORMATION

EMAIL- LEE CUMMINGS.....lee0260@comcast.net

MSGS- NEGRO QUESTION BOOKSTORE WEBSITE

LEAVE A MESSAGE ON THE CONTACT PAGE, LOCATED AT THE BOTTOM OF THE NEGRO QUESTION BOOKSTORE WEBSITE. EACH FIELD ON THE FORM MUST BE COMPLETED OR YOU WILL RECEIVE AN ERROR MESSAGE. THIS IS TRULY...THE NEXT EPISODE!